The Fool's First Steps
The True Nature of Reality

Chris Thomas

The Fool's First Steps
The True Nature of Reality

ISBN 186163 0727

First printed 1999
Reprinted 2001
Reprinted 2003

Cover design by Paul Mason
Cover illustration by Zee

Published by:

Capall Bann Publishing
Auton Farm
Milverton
Somerset
TA4 1NE

Contents

By the same author, also published by Capall Bann:

The Journey Home

The Healing Book (with Diane Baker)

Everything You Wanted To Know About Your Body, But So Far Nobody's Been Able To Tell You (with Diane Baker)

About the Book

We are at the mid point of the greatest transformation that has ever taken place in the history of the universe and it is we who are making this change happen.

All of us, at one time or another, has asked the same questions: who are we? Where did we come from? What is our purpose?

In this book, we begin to unlock the answers.

Included here is a framework into which all of our emerging memories can fit and help us to arrive at a greater understanding of humanity and our place in our world. This is the most amazing time in our history and all of these changes, the main steps along our collective path, are chronicled here.

Also contained within these pages is a brief history of the other universal races and the parts that they have played in helping humanity along its way. Many of the Earth's mysteries are also explained here in simple, uncomplicated terms which cuts through the clouds of mysticism and unlocks the simple truth.

"The Fool's First Steps" follows on from *"The Journey Home"* and explains some of its themes in more detail and delves much more deeply into human history and development. It also takes a step by step approach to people's personal changes and provides practical ways of dealing with some of the health and personal problems encountered along the way.

About the Author

The author lives in Exeter with his wife Diane where they run their psychic surgery healing practice.

The author also teaches healing, both for beginners and healers who wish to learn how to manipulate energy to begin to mimic "surgical" procedures.

He has worked as a healer and "medium" for over eighteen years and also works directly with the new ley line grid and energy centres and with the Faerie.

He is also actively working for tax exemption for chocolate.

Dedication

To all those who found the courage to take their steps.

And to Diane whose footsteps I can now walk with again into the ancient past that is also our present and future.

It is such a fine and easy thing, the truth. I don't know why we ever lost sight of it.

Anon

Introduction

Since the publication of "*The Journey Home*" there have been a large number of questions asked about who we are, where we came from and what is our purpose. There have also been a number of questions asked about some of the implications raised in terms of Earth energies and ancient sites.

In "*The Fool's First Steps*" we begin to look at these questions in more depth and begin to delve into the answers.

We are proving to be so much more than we have been led to believe and many of these answers are now available to us for the first time in seven thousand years.

The human condition is now, more than at any time in our history, one of rapid and accelerating change and the answers that come to light in our search for knowledge are becoming easier to obtain whilst at the same time more and more questions come to mind.

The answers provided in this book have been arrived at through several different sources. The author has worked for a number of years as a "medium" and began his researches into human history whilst working with a variety of sources over a period of several years. More recently, our growing levels of consciousness has allowed access into the memory contained within the "Higher Self" and very many of the answers to our questions can be found there.

There is also another level of memory that is becoming more easily accessible and that is the "Akashic Records". This source of information is, in fact, the human "Higher Self" or, more accurately, the collective mass consciousness. Access to this source is not denied to anyone, all that is required is the desire to question.

Enclosed in these pages is a step along the continuing path to full memory. There is contained within our consciousness many memories of many lifetimes which are slowly emerging into our conscious minds but are being falsely coloured by the experiences we have encountered in our current lifetime. Our DNA patterns (DNA is deoxyribonucleic acid and is the basic building block of the body and all of its cells) contain all of who and what we are, or have ever been, and as our DNA continues to alter and recombine many memories and old illnesses are being re-discovered and cleansed. We are currently undergoing our final cleansing and transformation and the pace of change is one of rapidly increasing acceleration.

To record a full human history would take several volumes and serve only academic interest. What is included here are the main change points and an explanation of the steps that led us there. There is also a closer look at those with whom we share this universe of ours and their role in shaping human history.

A further step along our path is an explanation of ancient sites and the energies contained within them. Over the centuries, these energies have been modified to suit our changing needs but, as we return to fuller understanding, we are returning to a situation where the original purposes for these energy points need to be re-discovered and put to their original uses. Some of the answers provided will be surprising and new whilst at the same time opening up old memories that have lain dormant and unused for many centuries.

But where did our journey begin? What were these fool's first steps and from where did those steps begin? Why did we make those first steps at all?

We are everything that we have ever dared to dream we are and considerably more. All that we now need to do is to take our dreams beyond our physical restrictions and encompass the stars.

Chapter One

The Beginning

It is the end of the twentieth century and we have walked a long and tortuous path to arrive at this time.

Gone are the builders of the pyramids, in all of their lands, and with them those who could understand their meaning. We stand on a radioactive refuse heap of our own making. The planet has reached the point when we are no longer able to undo the damage we have created. The pall of death and destruction pervades our every breath and our vision is clogged by the smoke from a thousand funeral pyres. The seas are throwing up their poisoned dead for our final inspection mourned by the echoes of the whales' song.

Such is the view of our world held by many.

But yet.

It is the end of the twentieth century and we have walked a long and tortuous path to arrive at this time.

The pyramid builders are returning. The crown chakra has begun to open and make our consciousness complete. The land has begun to swallow our mistakes and is helping to rebuild what once was. The death of many species has been overtaken by the re-emergence of the extinct. The fires of destruction lead to new growth and the seas bring forth their dead for us to grieve for our mistakes whilst harbouring new life and new growth in their hidden depths.

Such is the view of our world held by many.

We have arrived, but for the moment we are not sure where our journeyings have brought us. Our arrival on new old shores has, temporarily, made us lost.

Our universe is a vast space and our small solar system, that which we have come to know as home, occupies a very marginal position on the edges of the middle of nowhere. The location for our world was chosen for many reasons, one of which being that we were out of the main stream of the universal flow.

We exist on a world of very narrowly defined boundaries that have served to contain us. We look out to the stars but comprehend very little of what we see. We look to the planet and understand even less. We look at our bodies and see only flesh.

We are not this small. Circumstances and choices have brought us to this narrow view point and we are only now beginning to remember that we are more.

We are not a body that has a soul but a soul, an immense eternal consciousness, that has built for itself a body.

Our origins take us back to the formation of the universe itself and perhaps beyond even that. We have placed ourselves within our confinement in order to further available experience and to re-define the limits to life.

Our deepest memories contain the echoes of these choices and have become incorporated into the basic doctrines that underlie all of our religions:

We are of the Creator and, when our work is done, we will return to the Creator. It is what we do in the interim that will make the difference and that is entirely our free choice.

There is no good or evil, only life and our free choices that have determined that life. We freely chose to be here and be a part of our Earth, ever since it became habitable, and have freely chosen the routes we have taken ever since. The Creator has not interfered in our choices and does not interfere in our choices.

Life within the universe could be likened to baking a cake. All of the ingredients are mixed together and placed in the oven to cook for a particular period of time, we do not open the oven door every two seconds to see what is happening nor do we re-direct the movements of individual ingredients.

Within the realms of quantum physics there is a pre-generative condition which is described as "Fields of Possibility". This is how scientists describe the condition of existence prior to the "Big Bang". This is also a way in which the Creator could be described - a limitless energy source which incorporates the consciousness, and the will, to investigate every possibility that could exist.

Life begins with a curiosity for the possible.

Our universe contains all of the energy that is required for life and all of the possibilities that life is able to incorporate and investigate. This is our purpose, to freely choose to experiment with possibility.

Our universe was created for this reason.

All living things have a consciousness of one level of understanding or another. The universe itself thinks and comprehends and assists all other life forms to exist. This was the real beginning - the creation of the universe itself. For some it came with a "Big Bang" whilst for others it came with a "Divine Breath".

Whatever the views of the individual, consciousness arrived.

The "Universal Consciousness" contains all that is required for other free thinking, comprehending, forms of life to exist. Everything is energy. The universal envelope contains and is comprised of an effectively limitless supply of energy which can help to generate and sustain all of the forms of life that wish to be a part of that particular universal consciousness.

The primary frequencies of the universal energies are those which correspond to freedom of choice. This is the energy "signature" of our universe, the freedom to choose our existence and our part within the universal whole.

Everything that exists within this universe has this ability. Nothing is excluded from this energy or the available possibilities. All that is required is an understanding that the options are available.

Ultimately, everything is comprised of an energy. It is the frequency, or range of frequencies that determine the level of consciousness at which we exist. As the universal void began to fill with the energy potential for life, several of the newly created consciousnesses combined together to form the early galaxies and star systems in order to provide the beginnings of a structure. This is achieved by the consciousness, that is the star, compressing elements of its being into a definable form, in other words, matter. Once these galaxies began to form into definable structures the next stages of possibility were begun.

The consciousness that forms itself into a star contains the potential to generate and to sustain other levels of being. This is how all life begins its existence, it is generated by a larger consciousness as part of its own potential.

The first free moving, free thinking inhabitants of our universe were brought into being by a combination of two factors, the raw materials provided by the stars and the energy, the will, of the Creator providing the awareness and potential.

Life was created in six very diverse regions of the universe to provide characteristics for what amounted to six different races.

These races could not be described as physical. They are comprised of an energy which is not compact enough to provide a dense physical form but they do still have a definable outline which is essentially humanoid in shape.

These "entities" began their existence as six very different groups of individuals who inhabited regions of the universe that are very remote to each other. Each began to generate their own collective consciousness which meant that, although each individual could remain as an individual, they could also form a mass consciousness that included every single one of their race within which each could knowingly function. This meant that their knowledge and understanding could be shared by each individual and, as a race, could raise their total sum of knowledge very rapidly and effectively.

Their method of communication was what we would consider to be telepathy. This meant that each individual could "speak" to each other but also, through their mass connections, to the race as a whole. By developing this capability within their own race it also meant that they could transmit their thoughts across the spaces between galaxies and all six races very quickly knew of the existence of each other. These "Six Higher Civilisations" we know collectively as "Angels" and we will go on to discuss their role in human development a little later.

The successful integration of the Six Higher Civilisations had proved that this universe had the potential to support and nurture life and so it was decided, by the Universal Consciousness, to explore some of the other life potential that this universe contains.

The Six Higher Civilisations exist only as an energy, they do not have a solid form as we would understand it and a further stage of development could be achieved by generating frequencies of energy which created a density giving rise to "physical" matter.

By this stage, in the universe's development, some of the individual stars had experimented with condensing energy into a more "solid" structure that brought about planets.

Planets are stable platforms from which other, lesser, forms of life can begin to develop. The consciousness, that is a planet, has the capability of developing and generating species of flora and fauna. However, flora and fauna tend to contain sufficient levels of awareness where they are barely aware of their own existence and were, generally, unable to develop very far beyond this level by themselves.

This next stage of development was brought about by the Universal Consciousness and the Six Higher Civilisations working together to "develop" the most "promising" forms of life that existed on seven very different planets. The seven planets were chosen because their climates and their life forms were totally different to each other. These developed life forms are much closer to ourselves than to the Six Higher Civilisations in terms of energy density.

We will go on to discuss these "Seven Lower Civilisations" in more detail in chapter six.

Although these life forms were developed, or as we would describe the process, genetically manipulated, it was their physical bodies that were developed, their consciousness (or soul) still came from the Creator. These seven planets, and their newly generated life forms, now began to develop quite rapidly. However, they do not have the Six Higher Civilisation's range of psychic capabilities and have not developed a joint mass consciousness. "Physical" density can reduce the range of "higher" brain capabilities. They do, however, retain a telepathic ability and this is their primary means of communication.

It has been inhabitants of two of these seven civilisations that have been responsible for the majority of UFO sightings and abduction stories.

At the same time as the "Seven Lower Civilisations" were being developed, a further level of potential was being investigated at another location. This was not an eighth member of the lower civilisations but an entirely new form of life. If the work to bring about the seven civilisations was successful, then it should be possible to increase material density even further to a point where "full" physical life was possible.

A small star was just beginning to form itself and the consciousness, that was this star, was asked by the Universal Consciousness to investigate the creation of a solar system that was able to sustain many forms of life at, what was considered to be, an extremely dense level of energy compaction.

Thirteen individual planets were to make up this solar system each with its own consciousness and characteristics.

Each of the thirteen planets was given the task of developing flora and fauna that were best suited to their individual personality with the view to the possible future development of life forms which could accept and work with "full" consciousness. Full is used in the context of being free thinking, free acting and totally aware of their surroundings and their part within them.

The planets all began to settle into their own forms of expression and exploration. Each began to develop a suitable atmosphere and plant species that could sustain and enrich that atmosphere. Each planet generated its own particular mix of gases and ways of regulating temperature and life supporting organisms.

After a suitable period, the Universal Consciousness, together with the Six Higher Civilisations, began to collect together a variety of life forms from throughout the universe and genetically manipulate them into species that were best suited for each of the thirteen planets.

Each planet was seeded in this way. All thirteen developed and supported life and welcomed in and adjusted their eco-structures to accommodate these higher forms of life.

Life developed as a combination of creation, genetic manipulation and natural selection on all of the planets. Life at this physical a density worked and, left to their own devices for a few million years, produced a variety and abundance that was beyond all expectations.

Then there followed the next stage of the experiment - the introduction of life forms that had the capacity to develop the potential for "full" consciousness.

The seven lower civilisations, and the animal and plants with which they shared their home worlds, were made up of a large diversity of genetic forms which could lend themselves to further development and manipulation that would allow them to live and function at the extremely dense levels of existence that were required for these new planets.

Each of the thirteen planets had begun to develop their own free moving fauna and these were investigated for compatibility with the genetic structures of the life from the seven civilisations.

Each of the thirteen planets had their own structure, density and "personality" and the new forms of life were deliberately re-structured to suit a particular planet. All thirteen planets were newly seeded in this way and it led to a further stage of rapid development.

Each planet developed in their own ways and their flora and fauna, including the newly seeded species, took off in totally different directions and the diversity of life proved to be exceptional.

Three planets, in particular, showed an enthusiasm for life that outshone all of the others. Most had encountered problems with their eco-system balance that created problems which would prove, ultimately very difficult to overcome, but these three became exceptional in their variety of life forms and were encouraged to develop and progress.

These were the second, fourth and fifth planets from the solar system's sun. The second's primary life forms were small creatures that could be described as a blend of reptile and fish that spent half of their time in the planet's oceans and the other half roaming the giant forests that covered two thirds of the planet's surface. The planet's atmosphere was primarily made up of a gas similar to sulphur which to us would be extremely toxic.

The fourth's primary life forms were reptilian and massive and inhabited both the lands and the seas. The lands were covered in a large variety of plants and trees and had a range of temperature zones which added to the diversity of life forms. its atmosphere was primarily composed of carbon dioxide and nitrogen but with large concentrations of oxygen. its surface was about two thirds covered with water.

The fifth's primary life forms were primate like mammals of medium size, not unlike early humans. Their planet was mainly covered in tall grasses and short trees, although we would not recognise most of them as such and the planet did not have much surface water. its atmosphere was primarily carbon dioxide.

The other planets supported life in large quantities but, for many reasons, they were unable to sustain suitable forms of life that were able to take on higher levels of consciousness.

It can appear strange to talk of planets, galaxies, even the universe as having a consciousness that can think and act independently. We are used to believing that such structures are inanimate matter that follow some "natural law" or other. However, many now accept the concept of "Gaia" or Mother Earth and the implications of a planetary consciousness. It is this concept which is growing in acceptance and realisation and a growing number are beginning to take this on as a reality and to work with and within the planetary being.

What this concept implies is that planets are an independent life form within their own right and are able to make decisions about their own existence and the life that they develop and support.

This decision making process also includes the wish for existence in the first place, or as in the case of four of the planets in this solar system, the wish for continued existence.

When this solar system was formed it was asked to provide a place where high density "physical" beings could exist and develop into fully sentient beings. Some of these planets had encountered problems with fulfiling their chosen role and had decided to withdraw from the experiment.

The first planet choosing to take this course of action did so in a way which created many problems. Planets were a new way to fulfil a particular form of potential and their affects upon other planets in a particular solar system were not fully appreciated. Stars form and, ultimately, they collapse blowing their denser energies into the empty space around them whilst the consciousness leaves its "shell" in order to experience new possibilities. The denser energies are either re-used by the star's consciousness in forming a new "shell" or are distributed around the region of space and used by other consciousnesses for their own purposes.

Planets are usually a part of a star's consciousness and therefore remain in existence as long as the star does. In this particular solar system the planets were individuals who chose to take on their particular roles and, therefore, retained the capacity to think and act independently of the star.

The first planet to make this choice exploded. It was located between the second and fourth planets. Once this planet exploded the second one, to have made the decision to remove itself from the experiment, also exploded. This second planet was located between the fifth and seventh planets.

These explosions had a number of implications.

The first planet was thrown towards the sun and its rotation stopped, losing its atmosphere and all of its life forms.

The second planet was thrown off orbit and came very close to colliding with the fourth planet. its liquid core was thrown off balance which blew through the planet's surface destroying all life and heating the atmosphere to a point where it became unstable and collapsed in upon itself. It was also showered with a very large number of fragments of the third planet.

The fourth planet was rocked upon its equatorial axis and hit by two huge sections of the third and sixth planets. This tore away much of its atmosphere and destroyed many of the life forms upon the planet. It also plunged it into darkness caused by the vast amount of debris thrown into the much reduced atmosphere by the impact of the sections of the other planets. These impacts were also powerful enough to trigger many extremely large volcanic eruptions from deep within the planet's core. These lava flows covered huge areas of the planet and continued flowing for many centuries adding to the destruction of life. The planet also gained a moon.

The fifth planet was thrown off its orbit and ninety five percent of its atmosphere was blown off totally destroying all of its life forms and its surface was bombarded with the debris of the sixth planet.

The seventh planet suffered a major collision by most of the sixth planet which made it extremely unstable and to lose most of its physical cohesion. It also gained four moons.

The ninth, eleventh, twelfth and thirteenth were thrown into new orbits that were much further away from the star, destroying most of their life forms. The life forms that did remain slowly went into decline and now no life remains on any of these planets.

Two further planets within this solar system had also decided to remove themselves from the experiment for similar reasons to the first two. These were the eighth and tenth planets counted from the star.

Due to the disastrous nature of the removal of the first two, a gentler form of departure was devised for these two planets. Essentially the consciousnesses left their planets and the solid material slowly fell apart and disintegrated. Most of this debris was utilised by the star itself to reinforce its own structures and the remainder, together with the residue of the first two planets, collected together and formed a band of debris between the remaining fourth and fifth planets.

This now left nine planets within the solar system and the only two planets capable of supporting any kind of life was the third and one of the moons of the fifth.

We know these nine planets Mercury, Venus, Earth, Mars, Jupiter, Saturn, Uranus, Neptune and Pluto.

For the time being we will focus on the third planet, our home, the Earth, the life that still remains on Jupiter's moon, Gannymede, we will deal with in chapter six.

Life exists because it recognises the possibility. Once it has realised that potential, it becomes virtually impossible to deny it its existence.

Earth had sustained a massive blow to its life supporting potential. Most of the life forms that it had generated, or had welcomed in from other worlds, were now destroyed. Could the planet regenerate itself sufficiently to, essentially, begin again?

The potential for life had been realised and the planet was not intending to lose the joy that it had found in nurturing and supporting that life. So Earth began to re-build itself and to re-populate its lands and seas.

Away from the planet, a great deal of discussion was taking place about what to do next. Was the planet to be left to its' own devices and allowed to generate life forms that it considered to be appropriate? Should a new plan be formulated that took the development of this solar system in new directions? Should the original plan be re-started?

To complicate these issues, one of the seven lower civilisations had been the main donor of genetic material for the very successful large reptiles that had so recently been destroyed and saw the planet as their domain. Their view was that Earth was theirs and they should be the ones who inherited its' potential.

This debate led to many conflicts of interest and proved extremely difficult to resolve. For many, the memory of this debate has led to a belief that an inter-galactic war took place in early Earth history.

The concept of war is one which is uniquely human and, whilst this debate became very heated, no actual physical "war" occurred.

The debate was finally settled as a compromise.

The development of the planet was to continue, to produce a fully functioning, sentient, physical life form. A new higher life form was to be developed, but it was to share the planet with other forms of life which retained the genetic source material of the seven lower civilisations and were to be allowed to develop their own levels of conscious awareness in direct competition.

This "battle" of the species was to be waged over very many centuries. Essentially it was a war between reptile and mammal and the final winners were to inherit the Earth.

Chapter Two

The Dawning of Man

There remained one planet, out of the original thirteen, that was capable of supporting forms of life that could begin the process of developing a full state of consciousness.

Apart from one small, but bright, glimmer on an isolated moon, the other twelve planets were essentially devoid of all life.

So began the reconstruction of the Earth and the process of massive re-population. Not everything had been lost and many lessons had been learned, however, new life had to be found. The planetary consciousness had been responsible for generating many of the forms of flora and fauna that had existed before the destruction and it began to re-introduce some of the more promising developments.

Away from Earth, the search began anew for suitable life forms that could exist in this newly regenerated paradise. In finding suitable forms of life for the pre-disaster Earth, one of the seven minor civilisations had developed exceptional genetic manipulation skills. These skills had been utilised to modify the flora and fauna that had been chosen from other worlds, throughout the galaxy, and they were put into service once again to bring about a new rush of life. This civilisation had retained a large number of the genetic records of the species that had populated the solar system and these were investigated for their suitability for inclusion in the new ecological balance that was to emerge on Earth.

Three million years ago the "battle" for the inheritance of the planet had been won and the final "victors" were mammals.

In several aspects, the forms of life that had been developed on what was now the fourth planet, Mars, had progressed at a remarkable pace and were suitable for life on Earth in a virtually unchanged state. These were mammals who had begun to evolve into a form of primate and they were introduced to the planet. The planetary consciousness also began to develop primate forms of life and both of these groups were encouraged to progress.

This group of animals were encouraged for several reasons. Firstly, they were humanoid in form and more suited to the natural consciousness shape that had originally been created. Secondly, they tended to form naturally into "family" groups and showed the beginnings of a collective way of living. Thirdly, they were comparatively slow to grow into maturity and this could be used as a period where the young could be educated. Fourthly, their cell structures showed a tendency to easily absorb new information into their DNA, in other words they could learn both by experience and by example, and this could be used to rapidly enhance their development.

A number of groups began to emerge which showed these characteristics and potential for growth and development. They were to be found all over the planet but particularly in Africa, Australasia, Indonesia and South America. The loss of atmosphere and disruption to the planet's magnetic flux had resulted in very unstable weather patterns and these early primates required heat and concentrations of carbon dioxide to develop their mental functions. In the regions around the poles, high concentrations of oxygen tend to form over the colder air. Whilst oxygen is necessary for the life on Earth, carbon dioxide helps to promote rapid growth, particularly brain functions (too much carbon dioxide makes us lethargic, of course, and can slow down brain functions).

The current change in the global climate is a reflection of this requirement. Whilst our activities have generated many of the so called "green house gasses", it is the planet itself, responding to our need for change, that has produced approximately ninety percent of the gasses that increase the concentrations of carbon dioxide in the atmosphere, thereby promoting change within our brain structures. The mixture of gasses should reach a balance in 1999 which will be at the right concentrations to assist our brain activity.

The primates developed in temperate lands and slowly spread out across the whole planet surface as the weather patterns began to stabilise again.

Each group of primates was actively watched and genetic modifications were made in order to alter physical structures to make them more compatible with the planetary regions that were inhabitable. For example, an ability to withstand cold or greater lung capacity for mountainous regions etc..

Despite this help and encouragement, development of these primate groups was very slow and the causes were proving extremely difficult to find. The whole purpose of the development of these primate groups was to develop a "physical" body which could contain the full levels of consciousness. The slow progression of the evolution of these groups began to call into question the possibility of this goal being achieved. Many thousands of years had passed since the mammal groups had been seeded and the anticipated progress had not occurred so a change of approach was now required.

The locations of the continents, at this time, were not as they are now and there existed a large ice island approximately in the location of South America. This island was chosen as it was remote from the main areas where the primates were living and could therefore safely be used for a "research station". The station was manned primarily by the genetic manipulators who were one of the seven minor civilisations. We know this island land as Lemuria and approximately one hundred thousand years ago they began investigating primate development.

Lemuria existed for about six thousand years and totally fulfiled its function in determining the reasons for the slow rate of development. Primarily, the planet was experiencing its own problems since the loss of the other planets in the solar system. It was finding extreme difficulty in reaching a state of balance and consequently was generating major fluctuations in its magnetic field. These constant field changes were disrupting the flora and fauna, especially the primate's, energy patterns which stunted growth and development and radically altered the way in which DNA patterns developed. Other causes found were extreme weather patterns, particularly periodic icing of the planet's surface and relatively low temperature levels.

Essentially, the problem was not the primates but the planetary consciousness itself and work was begun to assist the planet to arrive at a more balanced condition.

This was the primary purpose of Lemuria, to assist the planet in achieving balance. its secondary function was to study the groups of primates and determine ways in which they could be assisted to achieve the ultimate goal of physical consciousness.

The work was carried out by two main groups. The planetary consciousness was assisted by the six major civilisations and the primates were studied by a member of the seven minor civilisations.

This work took about six thousand years to achieve and the planet was then left to its own devices for the next nine thousand years.

As the planet's weather patterns stabilised and temperatures began to rise, Lemuria gradually disappeared into the oceans. Lemuria had served its purpose and the planet, and its amazing variety of life, were now beginning to be understood. This kind of planet, and the life it supported, was entirely new. Life, at "physical" densities of energy, did not exist anywhere else throughout the universe and the way in which it would develop and respond was totally unknown. Physical life was known to be feasible, the dinosaurs had proven that, but a form suitable for full consciousness capability was totally new.

The results of the primate study showed that the anticipated development of a suitable body form, and DNA patterns, had been slowed to a point where the planned "human" was still in a very underdeveloped state and, at their current rate of development, would take a further one hundred to two hundred thousand years to arrive at a suitable level of readiness.

It was decided, by the universal consciousness, to accelerate this process by altering the DNA structures, of these primates, to arrive at the desired possible outcome much earlier than if the planet was allowed to act by itself.

A collective decision was made to return to Earth and establish a new "research station" on a large island in the Atlantic Ocean. This location was chosen as it represented an average of all of the climatic regions that then existed. The island stretched from Britain, in the north to Brazil, in the

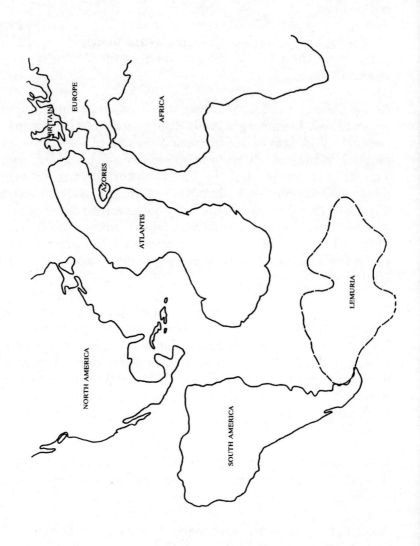

The World Map Showing Lemuria and Atlantis

south. South America was not located in its current position, but was much further out into the Pacific Ocean (see illustration number one).

We know this large island as the Continent of Atlantis.

Atlantis is an interesting part of our history. Memories of this time and place conjure up many images and recollections that vary considerably with each individual. For some it was a golden age, whilst for others it was a time filled with fear and loathing. All of these memories fit within the reality that was Atlantis, but they need to be put into context and into the correct time sequences.

Atlantis was first "colonised", as a "scientific" establishment, eighty five thousand years ago. The first members of the community were from a star system we know as NGC584, these were the "geneticists" who had set up the research facility on Lemuria. These first arrivals came in what we would describe as "space ships", a few of which crashed on arrival. The first buildings were located in the middle of the southern end of the island, on a flat grassy plain adjacent to a large lake. These first buildings were the beginning of an adventure that was, eventually, to span fifteen thousand years and was to begin human history and development. Our involvement with the planet could, and should, be measured from this time.

The whole purpose of Earth was to bring about individuals who were "fully" conscious and able to function within a physical body. This state of being had never existed before and every effort was to be made to bring this state of being into existence.

The work was begun by gathering together a group of representatives of each of the different types of primates that had begun to move away from their purely animal characteristics. These could not be described as human, but a species of mammals who had been encouraged to form into a humanoid shape, both by the planet and the six higher civilisations following their earlier seeding from other worlds, particularly from the pre-disaster Mars.

The genetic structures of these primates were altered and enhanced to bring about a rapid level of development. This was achieved by adding a form of micro-chip onto their spinal columns. In form and structure, these "chips" were very similar to the energy "barbs" still used by African tribal shaman for purposes that are not quite so positive as these.

This "chip" was programmed to read, monitor and work with the DNA of the host to accelerate the change of bodily structures, shape of head, nervous system and sensory systems to ultimately produce an erect, fully functioning, human body.

Although this is a process that sounds a little like the kind of genetic experiments that our scientists are currently involved in, and all of the horrors that those entail, they were not. These processes worked with the body in very positive and subtle ways which did not harm or cause any distress to the mammals involved.

Out of these initial enhancements came our direct ancestors. After only three generations, there now existed pre-human primates that were able to think and reason in several basic ways.

Once this stage of development was reached, all of the work was called to a halt and the enhanced primates were allowed to develop by themselves in their own ways and in their own habitats for the next one thousand years. This was to allow them to develop in their own ways and to reach their own levels of awareness that were their own natural levels. No further enhancements were to take place until these early humans were in a position to make a choice for themselves.

The prime directive of freedom of choice applies to all levels of life, if a form of life has a basic awareness of itself, then it must be allowed its own choices in all aspects of its life. This is why our scientific experiments, and treatment of animals, are so abhorrent to so many people, we have largely forgotten this fundamental "law". We act in ways which assumes a level of mastery over other living things and we forcibly inflict our will and ignore their choices.

The primates, that were a part of these enhancements, were a part of the planetary consciousness and were born of the planet for the specific purpose of developing into sentient beings. These new enhancements purely accelerated this development.

By helping these primates to develop an individual consciousness and break away from the planetary, mass consciousness, they were developing the beginnings of individual awareness, of a soul, and this began to put them into a position where they could choose for themselves.

This is where our own history and experiences begins to colour our view of Atlantis. Many of the memories that people hold of the type of work carried out on Atlantis, stems from a much later period when enthusiasm for experimentation led to some unacceptable mistakes.

The planetary development had been virtually stopped by an accident that was not of the planet's making. The removal of four planets had caused an enormous disruption to the Earth and all of its forms of life. What was being attempted here was to assist the planet in regaining much of the advancement that was lost due to the accident. A way of helping the planet to regain its own choices.

The loss of life, that had been brought about by this accident, had always been deeply regretted and this work was decided upon, by all of those involved, to attempt to undo some of the damage caused.

There then began the next stages of progression and these were begun in two different ways.

The early humans were now in a position where they could understand the choice they were now faced with. They could choose to continue their progression at their own pace and in locations on the planet where they would not be disturbed or interfered with in any way or, they could return to Atlantis and continue with the physical and consciousness enhancements.

It was an entirely free choice. It can be a little difficult for us, from our extremely cynical viewpoint, to accept that there are those who can act without any form of hidden agenda. If these early humans had chosen to develop at their own pace then, no matter what the aims of Atlantis were, they would have been allowed to do so and human development would have progressed at whatever pace it could without any attempts to artificially alter it.

The choice that was presented was made in a way that could be completely understood. The answers were mixed. There were choices made for both approaches and this is how the work progressed.

Those who wished to continue at their own pace were given free range of the planet and were left to be whatever they wanted to be in whatever way they chose, without interference.

The archeological records show how widely this branch of our ancestry roamed over the planet and the length of time that their descendants existed. Their history is well documented and their particular journeyings are outside of the scope of this book.

Those who elected to remain in Atlantis have a different history.

The work began with a continuation of the changes to their DNA structures. The body forms that had come out of the earlier enhancements were still quite crude and these were progressed until they quite closely resembled our own body shapes and structures. Eventually, after about four thousand years, a human emerged which had full consciousness capabilities. Although their body shape resembled our own, there were major differences.

The most important, and overriding, difference was the structure of their DNA. All life contains an encoding sequence that determines all of the bodily functions and capabilities. It also relates very closely to levels of consciousness. Our own DNA patterns contain many millions of these encoding sequences within a spiral that is made up of two separate, but intertwined, strands. In order to achieve "full" consciousness a minimum of seven of these strands are required. This high level of being was achieved by two means. Firstly, the capability was put into place by the genetic manipulations of the physical structures and secondly, an increasing level of consciousness was made available to them by the Creator.

So humanity was brought into existence in the same way as all life, a combination of Creation and evolution.

This meant that these humans were very much in advance of the humans we currently are. Their bodies were of a much lighter density, their psychic abilities were extremely advanced and their ability to absorb knowledge, and make use of that knowledge, was much greater than ours.

Through Atlantis, the universe had achieved its goal. A fully functioning, fully conscious physical being.

Humans had arrived on the planet.

For the next two thousand years humanity thrived and most of the universe came to visit and wonder.

Nowhere, within the whole of creation, did a planet such as Earth exist. its diversity and variety of life made it glorious. A new age had dawned and everything in the garden was wonderful. The Garden of Eden was very real and existed in the middle of the Atlantic Ocean.

The geneticists had also worked on all of the plants and animals that were on the island and they had achieved a state as close to perfection as it was able to physically achieve.

This is why, for some, our genetic memory of Atlantis is one of a "golden age". All things lived in total harmony, nobody needed and so nobody took. Everything that could possibly be needed for life was freely available. The lighter density of the body meant that heavy foods were not required. Sustenance was supplied by the free flow of energy between the planet and the people, solid food, when required, was picked directly off the abundant fruit and nut trees, or synthesized from a variety of sea weed. An ability to control local weather patterns meant that no one was cold or wet and so clothing was not required. Shelter could be made from branches and leaves and stronger, more permanent, buildings could be synthesized by machines or collectively built using a form of tele-kinesis. Energy requirements were supplied by utilising the energy of crystals which could also be psychically constructed and tuned.

Paradise had been achieved.

Atlantis was visited by many of the other races, especially the six higher civilisations. In order for them to understand what life on Earth was like, they needed to condense their own energies into a more physical structure and density, this process they found cumbersome and uncomfortable if they remained in this state for any length of time.

In order to experience what true physical existence was like they began to ask that they be born into a physical body.

This process might begin to sound a little like body snatching but it is, in fact, no different to the way in which we are born. We are a consciousness, a soul, that has built for itself a body. There are three individuals involved in this process, the mother, the father and the soul that is to begin its new life as a baby. Pregnancy occurs because these three individuals agree for it to occur, a form of pre-birth contract. The incoming soul wishes to be born and the parents agree to that soul being born to them (or, of course, the other way round where the parents wish for a child and the consciousness, that is to be that child, agrees to be born to these particular parents).

A number of the members of the six higher civilisations, or Angels as we would describe them, approached human females and asked if they could be born to them, as children, in order for them to experience full physical existence. Remember, this could not be experienced in any other location in the universe and was, therefore, of great interest to everyone.

So began a new phase of life on Atlantis. The process proved to be extremely successful and also extremely popular, both with the Angels and the human population. New experiences were being gained by everyone concerned and the whole process helped to raise the energy, and therefore consciousness, levels of the physical body. A human life time lasted for about nine hundred years, at this time, and frequently longer. The population was beginning to grow and spread out from the original settlement into the rest of the island and the first town was built. The whole population of Atlantis lived on the island, nobody lived on any other continent as this could interfere with those who had chosen not to be a part of the Atlantis enhancements. They could travel widely about the planet, usually by the process of translocation, but were very careful not to interact with the other inhabitants.

Gradually, more and more souls were born, a city was built and new energy structures were created to accommodate the increased requirement for "food". Nothing was done that could harm the planet or any of its inhabitants. Despite the large growth in population, Atlantis still remained a place of complete harmony.

Slowly, the situation began to change. Many of those who had experienced more than one physical incarnation began to experiment with other life forms. Was it possible to be born as a lion, for example. Could physical tissues from one animal be compatible with another to produce a new form of life? Was it possible to enhance certain physical characteristics in order to make some elements of the human body more suited to certain tasks or even to increase bodily sensitivities or pleasures?

There were those who began to think in this way and to experiment with these possibilities. Many experiments were carried out with varying degrees of success and practical applications and they began to become more and more bizarre. Only a small group of individuals were involved in these weird experiments, most preferred to enjoy life on Atlantis as it had been intended to live, as a natural, physical human.

It is the memory of these experiments that give rise to some people's memories of Atlantis being of a time of pain and suffering. It also is the reason why the current interest in genetic experimentation give so many of us the chills.

We all carry genetic memories of these experiments and it was an early attempt at purging these memories which resulted in many of these strange forms being painted or sculptured. Representations of these experimental forms are to be found all over the world, but particularly South America and Egypt where, in later times, they entered into the realms of religion and mythology.

Very many of us, who are currently living a physical life, were involved with Atlantis in a variety of ways. Those who were a part of the early life on Atlantis remember that time as being one of immense delight and joy in such surroundings. Those who were a part of the latter years of Atlantis can remember it as being a very dark and painful place.

It must be remembered that everything that we experience in a particular life time has been chosen by us to happen, nothing happens that we have not agreed to be a part of. Those who were a part of these horrendous experiments chose to be there. Some have accepted their mistakes and have attempted to point out to others that such experiments can lead to disaster and inappropriate actions. Many of these souls make up the ranks of anti-vivisectionists. Many others have remembered their part in these experiments and, whilst wishing to be a part of the current human transition, did not trust themselves to act responsibly in a human form and have, therefore, chosen to incarnate in a body form that cannot function as the human body does. Most of these have incarnated as dolphins. Then there are those who have memories of these experiments and wish to continue with their work.

Life on Atlantis was changing from a paradise to a very strange zoo. Attempts were made to limit these experiments and they were largely successful.

However, some of the research being carried out was for life that was destined for other planets. Many of the animals and plants, that had been developed for Earth, were also suitable, with minor modifications, for other worlds. One of these modifications went very wrong.

A bacteria had been developed which was destined for a world that did not contain much oxygen. This organism had the capacity to take in oxygen and convert it to hydrogen. On its destined home world, this function would prove to be extremely useful, but on Earth it could turn the planet into a wasteland totally devoid of all living things.

Somehow, this bacteria had entered into the machinery that synthesized the seaweed and had contaminated virtually all of the human, and part human, inhabitants of the island. Whilst their metabolism was able to deal with virtually any form of poison or contaminants, the bacteria was too slow acting to be immediately noticeable and it became very firmly established within the body before it was fully detected.

Try to imagine a situation where all of the body's oxygen, in every body cell, was converted to hydrogen. All of the body's water, seventy per cent of the body's volume, converted to hydrogen. This does not leave a great deal of physical tissue. The body reduces to a collection of crystals, not unlike salt.

The danger was that, if the bacteria was somehow carried to the rest of the planet, or allowed to mutate into a form that could migrate in the atmosphere, all life on the planet would be totally and completely destroyed. This had to be avoided at all cost.

Those who had not been contaminated, mainly non-genetically altered animals and those who had not been born as humans but remained as non-physical visitors, were removed from the island. The visitors away from the planet and the animals by craft to mainland Europe (the origin of the Noah's Ark story).

The rest had to decide what to do. The bacteria was, for the time being, confined to the island but it could begin to alter. The risk of possibly releasing a bacteria that was this dangerous into the planet's life, atmosphere and oceans could not be allowed to happen.

Earth had to continue, it was far too precious to risk its, potentially, total loss.

A collective decision was taken, by every soul involved, throughout the universe, to remove Atlantis from the planet's surface and Atlantis was deliberately sunk into the planet's magma core.

Chapter Three

New Beginnings

Atlantis was lost

The implications and repercussions were enormous. The destruction of Atlantis sent shock waves around the planet and far out into the universe. All life on the island had been lost. Everything that had been developed and stored had been destroyed. Virtually all of the genetic records of the whole of Earth's inhabitants, human and animal, were gone.

The affects on those who lived on the island were devastating. Almost all of the inhabitants had been killed. Those who were of the other civilisations had been able to cast off their physical bodies, so at least their consciousnesses, or souls, were intact, those who had been party to the most bizarre modifications were so tortured by their ordeals that they could not face any kind of continuation and had perished, including their souls, with the continent. This was also something new, no souls had ever been destroyed before.

The loss was total and the shock waves rocked the whole of creation.

The affects on the planet itself were equally massive. Although the planetary consciousness was part of the decision making process, to sink Atlantis, it could not predict, or prevent, all of the ensuing events from occurring.

Once the decision had been made to destroy the island, the whole of the inhabitants, together with the planetary consciousness, worked together to open up a large crack in the planet's crust.

The island was totally surrounded by volcanic eruptions which completely enveloped the island and its life, sealing them all into the rock (the origin of the Sodom and Gomorrah story). This level of destruction was required in order to minimise the possibility of any of the bacteria reaching any other living thing. The volcanoes then collapsed in upon themselves drawing the island into the planet's magma core. The resulting scar forming the mid Atlantic Ridge.

Opening up such a huge gap had very far reaching affects on the rest of the planet's surface.

All of the continents were affected in one way or another. The largest movement was in South America where the continent moved from being an island in the Pacific to its current location. A fault line opened up, from the mid Atlantic Ridge, through the straights of Gibraltar and turned a large marshy swamp into the Mediterranean Sea (the origin of the story of the flood).

The Caribbean basin was formed, the Great Rift valley in Africa was opened, Greenland and Iceland were separated and many of the planet's volcanoes were activated.

All that remained of Atlantis were three islands. These remained as they were the three primary energy supply points and were the main energy "interchanges" for the whole of the planet's ley line grid system. One of these islands, the Azores, had been mostly destroyed and was, therefore, abandoned. The remaining two, Britain and Ireland, and their role in future events, will be discussed later.

All that remained of human life were the pre-human primates who had decided not to take part in the Atlantis enhancements.

Seventy thousand years ago, these primates were capable of using stone tools, but little more, and lived primarily in cave shelters. They had the rudiments of language and were beginning to plan their actions before a situation arose, instead of being surprised into action - the start of collective reasoning.

They had been left totally to their own devices and had not been interfered with in any way, apart from an occasional visit to check on their development.

Fifteen thousand years had elapsed since the establishment of Atlantis and the progress of this other branch of humanity had been painfully slow.

There was now the question of what to do next. Was Earth to be abandoned to its own devices? If left alone, could these pre-humans develop into fully aware individuals? Should a new Atlantis be established? If so, would the lessons learned from the old Atlantis be enough to stop a similar accident occurring? What would the response of the pre-humans be if a new Atlantis was developed?

The answer was the same as committees the universe over. Wait and see.

Twenty eight thousand years ago, forty two thousand years after the destruction of Atlantis, a "delegation" came to Earth to speak with the members of the early human primates who had slowly developed along with the planet.

These visitors were members of the six higher civilisations who came to ask if several areas of the planet could be designated for use by the six higher civilisations to begin a new phase of development for a fully conscious physical being. This was not to be a re-run of the Atlantis experiments, but a totally new approach.

At this stage, these early humans had moved away from cave dwelling and had moved onto the plains as hunter gatherers with the beginnings of using farming and basic tools as well as a growing understanding of metals. Their levels of reasoning were developing rapidly and they were able to fully understand what was being asked of them. The visitors had also adopted a human density so as not to alarm the inhabitants.

Permission was given for the visitors to make use of certain areas which would not interfere with the development of the early human inhabitants.

A new Atlantis was not to be built, but separate areas of the planet were to be "seeded" with new "humans" to begin a new phase of development.

In order for this new "experiment" to take place, the energy structures of the planet needed to be adjusted and repaired following the damage created by the destruction and removal of the original energy source and grid that had been a part of Atlantis.

New global energy centres were put into place and a ley line network was constructed over the whole of the planet's surface. This work was carried out by an individual who has appeared at several times during human history to adjust energies and to aid progression. His work has been noted by several tribal traditions all over the world, he has also been known by a number of names, in South America he was known as Zamna, and incorrectly remembered as Quetzalcoatl, but his most well known is that of "The Merlin". This is, and always has been the merlin's role, not magic or conjuring tricks, but connection and adjustments of the energy matrix.

These energy adjustments were necessary to accommodate the chakra systems of the soon to be seeded humans. The existing inhabitants of the planet, plant, animal and early human, would not be adversely affected by this energy change, but could be helped by it themselves. At this point in Earth history, the seven chakras of the human body did not exist. All life on the planet had similar energy structures contained within their bodies. Most animals currently have three chakras, some larger animals have four and the human population has thirteen (seven physical and six non-physical). Twenty eight thousand years ago, animals had their three chakras and the human primates had four functioning chakras (root, second, fourth and seventh) and the three other physical chakras were gradually beginning to form.

By adjusting the planet's energy matrix, it would provide suitable energy levels for the soon to arrive humans, whilst at the same time maintain the existing inhabitants' energy requirements and provide the opportunity for these energy levels to be raised.

This was not intended to be interference with the planet's inhabitants, but an attempt to help everyone develop at a more rapid pace.

Twenty thousand years ago the first of the "new humans" arrived.

Six regions of the planet were chosen for this new beginning. These were: South America, Mesopotamia, Egypt, a region that included parts of Britain, Ireland and Northern France,

Tibet and Southern Greece. The last one of these regions, Southern Greece, no longer exists intact. This part of Greece was originally much larger until volcanic activity buried much of this region under the sea, leaving only a scattering of islands.

The regions listed are given in order of importance as the six higher civilisations judged them.

The new humans arrived as an energy form which they slowly condensed, mainly by using materials from the planet itself, into a "physical" body (the origin of the Adam and Eve story).

This new physical form allowed them to function as "full" physical beings. By incorporating the Earth's material, such as soil, into their physical constructions, it allowed them to familiarise themselves with the planet and their surroundings very rapidly. Any material could be used in this process. It was a question of re-forming the atomic structure of the chosen material into the required density and molecular build up.

It also meant that they were totally acclimatised to their region of the planet.

As with Atlantis, their material requirements were very low. Their main source of nourishment was the planet's energy matrix, with the occasional supplement of fruits, berries and nuts. They did not require any shelter as they were totally at home in their chosen environments.

Their life was one of exploration. Everything was new and exciting. Like children, given a new toy, they could hardly contain their joy and enthusiasm. All of life was open to them. They could "speak" freely with all life and understand its needs and wants.

They could travel freely about the land and the planet by a process that we would call translocation. Communication was by psychic means, both amongst each group or across continents. They had a life span in excess of one thousand years.

All of these groups remained quite small, two hundred in the smallest and five hundred in the largest, a total of two thousand one hundred and fifty over the whole planet.

There were six groups in total and each was made up of members of one of the six civilisations, the seven lower civilisations were not represented. It had been members of some of the seven lower civilisations, born into a human body, who had been responsible for most of the less than useful and bizarre genetic experimentation on Atlantis. In order for their lives and forms to be compatible with all other forms of life on the planet, they had taken on the roles and functions of being either male or female. This allowed for, when the time was deemed to be right, reproduction.

This aspect, of physical life, was something which the six higher civilisations were very unsure of. Most life, throughout the universe, have their own ways of reproducing which do not quite match our version and it was seen as a subject that should be approached with caution. The problems, that had been encountered at the end of Atlantis, weighed very heavily in the collective memories of the six higher civilisations. Should those who wished to partake of physical life build their bodies anew, as they arrived on the planet, or should the self replicating reproductive system, that was usual on the planet, be adopted?

Eventually, after about two hundred years, the matter was resolved by the adoption of sexual reproduction and the first new humans were born onto the planet by their human/angel mothers.

The population rose slowly and they continued to interact with the planet and all of its life without any kind of interference or harm. This was a truly golden age of complete harmony.

As life went on, they began to find new ways of working and interacting with the planet and with those who wished to visit. There was very keen interest by the six higher civilisations in these new inhabitants and the ways in which they fitted in with the planet and with their surroundings. The process of travel, from the home region of the six to Earth, was quite cumbersome. It meant that these beings needed to slow down their own energy frequencies to come closer to the vibrational level of the solar system and the planet. This is a process that would be like us trying to squeeze ourselves into a pint bottle. It was therefore decided to begin to develop "gateways" that would make travel much easier. These "gates" could also be used by the physical humans to briefly travel back to the realms of the six.

Several different types and forms of gateway were experimented with to see which could serve its function best. The first two gates were constructed with surrounding and insulating structures as a precaution against affecting the planet's own energies. These first two gates were at Teotehuacan in Mexico and the Sphinx in Egypt. They represented a new phase of development and are the first structures built by humans that were not built in Atlantis.

A second phase of experimentation was at Stonehenge. This gate was built without any form of surrounding or insulating structure and formed the model for all subsequent gates.

Following Stonehenge, all gates were built without any form of surrounding structure. Stone circles etc. were only added as our energies were in decline or they were added at a much later date for other purposes.

The other "gateways" were: in Tibet, on the Plateau of Tibet, North of the town of Gorno, now in China; in Mesopotamia, East of the town of Al Daghgharah, now in Iran; in Greece, this "gate" is now lost but was close to the island of Kolpos.

What these gateways represented were a direct link with our "home" worlds, those of the six civilisations. Although modified over the centuries, they still exist. The interest, and the recent work carried out on Stonehenge, for example, show that we are still capable of recognising these energy "gates".

Essentially, what we had provided was a "shuttle" service between our world and our home worlds. These links still exist. Energy cannot be destroyed, it can only be altered. Over the intervening centuries, these vast energy "doorways" have been utilised by those who can still operate them to keep a close eye on and to assist human development. Human use of these "gates" has been severely limited by the change of these energies by those who wish to hide our true potential and true origins.

The use of these "gateways" meant that the six higher civilisations, the Angels, could visit, and interact directly, with their physical brothers and sisters, and monitor progress on Earth, without the need for any uncomfortable transitional stages.

Very slowly, and almost unnoticed, the situation began to change.

We had arrived on the planet as "complete" human beings. A physical body with total conscious awareness.

The changes, to our situations, were very slow to arrive and, once they had begun to happen, were not easily recognised.

The planet itself has an energy. The energy can be compared to the body's aura and is distributed around the planet by a series of "meridians". There is another level of activity which is generated by the planet's core and could be likened to the body's biochemical signals. This energy manifests itself as an electro-magnetic field (the planet's energy structures do not actually act in the same ways as the human body's. It is only compared in this way to illustrate a particular point).

What this means is that all life on the planet is subjected to a constant stream of energy that has a frequency that is compatible with the life forms that had evolved with the planet. The recently arrived humans had a different frequency, one which was not totally compatible with the planet itself. Although they were perfectly matched, genetically, with the planet, their energy frequencies came from the realms of the six higher civilisations. These two energy structures, and their inherent range of frequencies, were to prove fundamentally incompatible.

The planet's "aura" and electro-magnetic field both have a frequency which resonates at about 8 Hz, or cycles per second (actually 7.56 Hz). This is the lowest end of the planet' energy emissions which then rise to many thousands of cycles per second. The new humans, because of their origins, had an energy frequency that began at 75 000 Hz, ten thousand times higher than the rest of Earth's inhabitants.

This all begins to become very technical but what it actually meant, for these new humans, was a gradual, but constant, slowing down of their natural resonance.

Although the planet's energy levels had been enhanced to accommodate the new humans' higher energy frequencies, the lower, base band of energy frequencies had to remain in place as the planet's life needed these frequencies to maintain their own connection with the planet. To exist on the planet, these new humans had taken on substance that contained these lower frequency ranges and their own, higher frequencies began to slow down to match those of the planet.

This slowing down began to manifest itself in many ways. The ability to translocate and bilocate began to be lost, many of the psychic communication abilities began to slow, travel to the home of the six became increasingly difficult, communication between continents was gradually lost, and there were many more symptoms that only became apparent as they became lost. The human world was slowly beginning to disintegrate and fragment.

Gradually, over a period of several thousand years, we were slowly becoming the same as the pre-human primates that had been originally seeded onto the planet.

This does not mean to say that they were taking on their physical characteristics but their energies were slowing down to a point where they were rapidly losing their higher energy connections and, therefore, many of the higher brain functions.

The reasons for so many of the problems encountered by these primates, and even all of the problems that had brought about the destruction of Atlantis, were beginning to become clear. It was the planet, the densities at which physical life existed, that was the root cause.

Higher energy frequencies, and therefore, higher consciousness abilities and frequencies, were not automatically compatible with the energies that corresponded to full physical life.

This was totally new information and time was needed to understand the implications more fully. Could fully conscious life really exist at fully physical levels? Would the planet have to be abandoned once again to its own devices and evolution with the hope that the pre-human primates could develop the hoped for levels of consciousness?

All of the new humans left the planet whilst these issues were being resolved. Fifteen thousand years ago we were once again back to square one.

When all of the new information was put together, a new "plan" was formulated. A new approach was needed where all of the potential pitfalls and problems encountered with the energy frequencies of physical life could be studied and used to the best advantage.

Up until this point, it had been assumed that any of the higher energy forms of life could adapt themselves to any situation and overcome any restrictions and problems. Earth, and its inherent energy frequencies, had proved that these assumptions were not necessarily correct.

On the face of it, these views can seem to be one of arrogance. Our universe is one where the freedom of choice is absolute. Anyone can be whatever they choose to be, without restriction. All of the forms of life, throughout the whole universe, exist because individuals have chosen to express themselves in a particular way. Every form of life has a consciousness, a soul, that exists across many dimensions and has a vast energy potential because of that multidimensional existence. The individuals who comprise the six higher civilisations have the capability of communicating with all of the many life forms that exist throughout the whole of the universe and have the capacity to "clothe" themselves as virtually any life form. To find that difficulties existed, of the type experienced on Earth, took them completely by surprise.

Investigations and discussions took place on very many levels and a new approach was decided upon which would include the pre-human primates that had been slowly developing and evolving by themselves. Again, there was complete freedom of choice. No situation was forced upon anybody, primate or Angel.

We are an energy, a consciousness, no more than that. What makes us, humanity, different is that we have chosen to clothe that energy in a dense physical shell that we call a body. We are a consciousness, a soul, that has a body.

The pre-human primates that existed on Earth at this time were a little different. They had been "seeded" on to the planet as part of an earlier wish to find suitable forms of life that could exist at what were considered to be extremely dense, physical levels of existence. This was a process of genetically manipulating suitable life forms from other worlds. In this instance, primarily pre-catastrophe Mars.

These primates were a part of the planetary consciousness in the same way as all plants and animals are but which, it was hoped, had the capacity to move away from the planetary consciousness and exist independently as free thinking, free acting fully sentient beings who could develop the capacity for "full consciousness".

The progress of these primates, to achieve independence, had been steady but extremely slow. Several groups had been helped to progress a little more rapidly, at their request, but in overall terms they were a long way away from achieving their goal.

Three options were now considered as the best way forward.

1. To return to Earth and begin again with the new humans but with the new knowledge that had been gained from the recently abandoned "new beginnings".

2. To return to Earth and begin to help the pre-human primates to progress more rapidly in ways which could not lead to the mistakes made in the later years of Atlantis. The primates would be fully consulted in ways which would allow them to make their own free choice.

3. A combination of both approaches.

An option to abandon the Earth had been considered but discounted. The life on Earth was considered too amazing and precious to be put into a position where it could be potentially lost.

In the end, option three was considered the most appropriate. This could be considered the real beginnings of what could be called "The Human Plan".

"The Human Plan" is essentially simple. The members of the six higher civilisations, who had chosen to be a part of the plan, were to work with the planet and all of its forms of life to determine a way in which full consciousness could be achieved. The plan could be modified and adjusted, or even abandoned, along the way as new information was gathered and understanding grew. This was essentially to be a co-operative. All members of this co-operative were to take on particular roles and to arrive at the completion of the plan at the same time. A time limit was set which reflected the time frame within which the work could be carried out and which also utilised a natural cycle of energies.

The galaxy, which contains Earth, has its own cycles of movement and change. A new phase of this cycle had begun at the time when the new humans first arrived on the planet (5,000 years previously). This cycle would last for twenty thousand years when the energies would once again change. The intention was to complete "The Human Plan" at the time when the galactic cycle began to enter a new phase so that the fully conscious, physical, mankind could use this new energy to move themselves forward into a new phase of development. Using the way in which we measure time, this twenty thousand year cycle comes to its end in the year 2011 and a new cycle begins.

Twelve thousand years ago the plan began. It was to operate in two ways. The angels, members of the six higher civilisations, were to arrive in the same way as they had eight thousand years previously and adopt a dense human form by taking in material from the planet itself. The pre-human primates, with their own free choice and cooperation, were to take on new energies and new genetic information to help accelerate their development. Both groups were to work very closely together to bring about a greater understanding of the way in which the planet, its energies and its densities functioned.

The work on the pre-human primates did not involve any kind of surgical procedures but took the form of "shifts" in energy frequencies which naturally modified their physical structures by working through the body's cell structure and DNA. The energies of both parts of the plan began to change. The pre-humans began to move forwards very rapidly and the new humans began their anticipated slowing down.

There is, of course, a third element to the plan and that is the planet itself. its part in "The Plan" was to maintain the plants and animals whilst they also underwent their own change as the energies of both elements of humanity began to alter the energies that were available on the planet.

Up until this point, human history had been primarily to do with our consciousnesses, our souls, taking on various suits of clothes to find a new kind of fit. Twelve thousand years ago, a new phase of development was begun which leads very directly to us and modern, recorded history now begins.

Chapter Four

The Karmic Cycle

Thirteen regions of the planet were chosen for this new wave of change. They are listed in no particular order :

South America, North America, Australia, Sumeria, Egypt, China, Asia (mainly India), a region that encompassed Britain, Ireland and Northern France, Indonesia, Pacific Islands (Polynesia), Scandinavia and Poland/Czechoslovakia. This is modern man and our beginnings.

Not all of the inhabitants of these lands were to be assisted in these ways. Freedom of choice remained as the determining factor in all situations. There were groups of individuals, on each continent, who had decided not to be a part of these changes. The wishes of these groups was honoured without exception and these tribes remained apart from the new humans until they chose to make a change.

This situation continued up until the present time until these isolated tribal groups chose to be discovered by travellers visiting their traditional home lands. Awareness of the current level of change is universal and many of the tribal peoples wish to be a part of the new global situation, this is why so many isolated peoples have been discovered since the beginning of this century.

The role of the new human groups was to assist and educate the primate humans to progress and develop in their own ways and to develop their own characteristics.

This was to be achieved by a variety of means and was to be constantly monitored and adjusted to suit each individual within each individual group. There was not to be any single way of achieving these goals, all were to be accepted and treated as autonomous groups and progress was to be made at a pace and in directions that were dictated by the individuals of these groups.

The work was begun in a variety of ways with each group.

Up until now these primate humans were essentially a part of the planetary consciousness and, therefore, only capable of thought and actions within their group, or mass, consciousness. The purpose of "The Human Plan" was two fold; to produce a fully functioning, conscious, being who could act in their own right, independently of the planet and secondly, to accelerate these new individuals to a point where "full" consciousness integration was possible.

The first stages of the work was to alter the cranial structures, to accommodate a larger, more complex brain and also to adjust the rest of the skeleton into a more upright stance. These stages were achieved by adjusting the primary DNA sequences by the addition of what could be described as accelerator genes.

These "accelerators" formed a "closed loop programme" which worked with the bodily structures gradually building upon pre-programmed goals. Within three generations, about one hundred years, we changed from a characteristically primate, near ape like, form into the form that we are today.

Again, each of the thirteen groups moved at their own pace and in the directions which they chose to go, nothing was forced or insisted upon. Each group determined their own final form and the speed of progress. This process was not like the genetic experiments which were carried out towards the end of the Atlantis period, but a method of gently enhancing that which already existed.

Once a more suitable body form existed, the second phase began. This was to bring about a higher level of consciousness that was independent of the planetary, primate, mass consciousness.

All of the plant and animal life that exists on any planet is essentially a part of the planet itself. The consciousness, the soul, that is the planet has the capability of generating and nurturing life in the form of plants and animals. In the case of Earth, this nurturing, generating capability was particularly well developed to allow for the amazing diversity of life that the planet supports.

In order to achieve diversity, the planetary being generates an energy form that a particular animal or plant is to take which incorporates all of the genetic material that is required for that particular animal or plant to become physical.

In other words, there is a grass energy form, a sea urchin energy form, an elephant energy form etc. which exists before the plant or animal can take on a physical existence. As a plant or animal takes on physical shape this energy form is kept as a template for other plants or animals that are to be generated as this particular family of animals or plants. Although each plant or animal has its own physical body and is able to grow and, in the case of animals, move in its own way and with apparent independent thought, they all share a common energy template which amounts to a mass consciousness.

Each plant and animal acts within, and can influence, its own group but will, usually, not affect other animal or plant groups. There are, of course, exceptions to this "rule". Particular plants or animals can act with each other to produce variations which can benefit those concerned. For example; some plants have altered their structure and their reproductive methods to suit particular animals who can provide a better method of fertilization or seed distribution, in return, the plant provides a type of food which the animal needs or particularly enjoys.

A new energy template was created, by the planet, with the assistance of the six higher civilisations, which was exclusively for the new human form. This separated us totally from the other primate groups. This had two benefits, one, we could not be tempted to experiment with producing a hybrid human/primate cross and two, we could develop at a more rapid pace to achieving independence from the planetary mass consciousness. This second benefit did not mean that we were to become totally separate from the planet but simply that we could evolve at our own, more rapid pace than the planet alone could provide.

This last change essentially produced a new species which was totally independent from any other species on the planet and allowed us to progress at a considerably higher rate of acceleration.

A secondary affect of producing an exclusively human energy template was that most of the tribal groups, who had decided not to be a part of the main work, began to take up the concept of a separate energy template and sub groups were formed which had their own new template and mass consciousness which were very similar to the new human form. These sub groups gradually changed and evolved into the new human form but also maintained a much closer connection with the planetary consciousness. These are the tribal groups who have maintained their distance from the, so-called, developing world by living out their lives in isolated regions of the planet.

By, about, eleven and a half thousand years ago, we were beginning to become one humanity. We all shared a body form and a common mass consciousness independent from all others. With the continued assistance of the Angels, the six higher civilisations, we began to develop in other directions.

The first of these was language. Up until now, we had communicated in gestures and crude vocalisations to express our wants and ideas. As we began to change from primate to human, our brains had developed to a point where we were able to think in more precise ways that could also encompass abstract thought.

All of the other races, throughout the universe, communicate by thought. This is a means of directly transmitting concepts, ideas and sensory information in a single thought. The closest analogy would be the transmission of television pictures. Sound and visual images are condensed into electronic impulses which are transmitted through the atmosphere. They remain as electronic impulses until someone tunes into the signal's frequency and the signals are converted back into sound and vision by the television's reception decoder. This is, essentially, how thought wave communications work. Communication centres within the brain "transmit" all of the required information directly into the brain of the individual that the transmission is aimed at. The recipient's brain then "decodes" these impulses back into thought, sound, smell, touch etc. This is why the Search for Extra Terrestrial Life (SETI) program has been unsuccessful in detecting radio wave transmissions from other regions of the universe, thought waves do not generate wave patterns that can be detected by our receivers.

At this time, we were not able to use this form of communication as the centres in the brain which transmit thought waves were not sufficiently developed.

We live on a planet that is filled with sound. The density of the atmosphere makes it ideal for the transmission of energy waves that translate into sounds. Our lives as primates had sharpened our hearing to a point where we could differentiate between a huge variety of sound sources and could, therefore, be tuned to accept sounds that represented thoughts.

Each of the thirteen groups were encouraged to develop a range of sounds that represented objects, animals, landscape, the weather etc. that could form the basis of language within each group.

From these basic beginnings, a huge complexity of language developed which also aided the progression of consciousness adaptation and development.

For some of the groups, this was sufficient for their needs and their purely verbal traditions continued for many centuries. For other groups, they required other ways of communicating ideas and a way of enhancing memory by a more tangible form.

The earlier "caveman" stages of our development had produced the use of symbols to represent objects, people or animals and so the concept of painted symbols as a form of language was understood by all. This understanding was developed, by some groups, to create a written form of their new spoken language.

Eleven thousand years ago the first written word appeared on the planet and was developed by the group of people who were to become the Hebrew.

These early, written, forms of language were modifications of simple forms, usually vertical lines that were crossed by horizontal or angled lines. Gradually, new types of symbols were added and developed which began a move to more complex forms, such as Egyptian hieroglyphs.

These written languages were developed from the types of symbols used by the other universal races. All symbols contain an energy. The act of impressing a symbol into another material imbues that symbol with the energy of the thought that went into creating it. This is how written language was originally intended to be used. Thoughts were focused into a symbol which, when read correctly, recreated those thoughts in the mind of the reader. They were literally a form of active memory that could be tapped into whenever that thought, represented by the symbol, was read.

This is how hieroglyphs should really be viewed. They cannot be taken as purely written images, but as symbols which represent a whole range of sensory information which we have, generally, forgotten how to interpret correctly. The process of imprinting these images into the stone they are carved upon, also holds the generating thought in place. A process very similar to that of succussing remedies used in homeopathic medicine.

These two developments, language and writing, gave us the beginnings of a unifying culture. We began to understand and to make ourselves be understood.

From these steps also came the sense of a shared existence, a belonging to a whole. When we had lived as pre-human primates we had lived in "tribal" communities, but these were usually a collection of individuals who only worked together for individual gain. By developing a common language we had made the step towards a co-operative community where each individual could feel a sense of belonging.

From these first steps there eventually came civilisations.

We were now ready for the next phase of our development. We had made many choices on our road to physical consciousness, some good, some not so good and some disastrous. Never the less, we were now at a stage in our progression where the beginnings of our goal could be seen.

Several problems still had to be overcome. The planetary energies had the capacity to reduce our level of awareness back to that of the primate groups from which we had so recently moved away. This potential problem was still to be properly solved.

Those of the six higher civilisations who had taken on physical form and matter were continuing to experience difficulties in maintaining their full levels of consciousness. They had discovered that the only effective way to deal with this difficulty was to periodically leave the solar system and return to their home regions for rest and recuperation.

The planet's energies were seen as the major stumbling block in the whole process.

It would be simple enough to alter the planet's energy fields to accommodate the changing rates of awareness of the human-primate groups but this would mean that most of the planetary generated life would disappear as they could not accommodate a change of energies of that magnitude.

In many ways, there was a simple choice to be made: proceed with "The Human Plan" by raising all of the planet's energies to a more suitable level and effectively destroy all other life or find a way to work within the planet's energies and still achieve the ultimate goal.

Put into these terms it can be seen that there was no real decision to make. The planet's other forms of life were far too precious to risk losing in this way and, therefore, "The Human Plan" must accommodate these constraints or be abandoned.

As a way of investigating this particular problem, a new form of development was begun. The human body form, that now existed, was capable of accommodating a higher form of consciousness and several of the Angels that had been working with the primates asked for permission to be born to human-primate parents. In this way, they could gain full experience of what the developed body was capable of and also begin to work with the planet's energy matrix from a position that was much closer to that of the planet.

The birth process mentioned is exactly the same as we still use. An incoming soul, the one who wishes to be born, approaches its potential parents and asks that those parents allow it to be born to them. The parents have the choice of accepting this particular soul or not. If negative, the soul finds other suitable parents, or, if affirmative, an agreement is made. This is essentially how all of those wishing to experience a physical life fulfil their wishes. Every situation has freedom of choice. The parents make their choice and the soul who wishes to be born has their choice.

So, the members of the six higher civilisations, the Angels, began a new cycle of human birth and experience.

Each of the thirteen groups were asked if they would accommodate this request and ask for volunteers who would act as parents to these children. No action would have been taken if any of these groups had denied access to the birth process.

There were a number of advantages to these children being born to human-primate parents. They learned directly how the human body developed, through its many phases. Up until now, the development process could only be observed. They learned from the inside how the tribal structures and beliefs were partly learned and partly genetic. Were further modifications required to the human body form energy model? There were also many more subtle pieces of extremely important information that could not have been arrived at by any other means.

The parents of these children also learned a great deal. These primate-humans gained their consciousness from the human mass consciousness and were not aware of the true differences between a mass awareness and the awareness of a "full" individual.

As these Angel/humans became to be more accepted by the thirteen groups, there was an increase in the number of volunteers who were willing to be the parents of these children. Gradually, more and more of these children were born, at the request of the tribes, and this eventually led to a situation where a majority of the people were of this type.

This situation led to a major dilemma. The goal of a fully conscious, physical being was being achieved at the cost of a loss of the primate-human population. Would it be better if the process was stopped or should it be allowed to continue to the point where the new conscious human was the only human form within the thirteen groups.

The final decision was eventually made by the primate-humans themselves. Their existence was as a part of a mass consciousness and, regardless of the final outcome of "The Human Plan", this mass consciousness would always remain a part of human existence. So these people saw an opportunity for greater growth, by all human beings, by the full integration of an "angelic consciousness" into a human body.

Again, we have a situation that begins to sound like a process of body snatching. The decision, by the primate-humans was made by themselves when they realised that this integration process could lead to a rapid change of condition to the developing humans and to the planet itself. There would also be advantages to the groups who had decided not to take part in the enhancement procedures.

These groups existed because the energy template, that gave physical matter its human shape, would be subtly altered by these changes as it would alter to the new consciousness form. This gave these other tribes a greater number of options: they could remain as they were and continue their own development in their own ways or they could undergo all, or part, of the same enhancement procedures. All options, and the choices inherent in those options, were still fully available to all of the human population.

We remember all of these events in two ways. Our DNA contains all of the genetic information that made up these primate-humans, their complete race memories and the memories of their bodies still give us our basic physical structures. Secondly, they are fully a part of the human mass consciousness and the memories that it contains. It has been necessary to edit these memories as space will not permit a full telling of this part of their history. Accessing the mass consciousness, for this particular time period, will reveal a greater depth of detail than has been included in these pages and show that these people still exist in a very real sense.

During the intervening centuries, the primate-human groups, that decided not to take an active role in these enhancement phases of our development, have also had their role to play. They have, at various times, decided to give birth to "angelic" children. These births have helped them to understand themselves, and their role on the planet, to a much greater degree. So, although they have remained largely apart from the bulk of humanity, they have taken on a role of guardians of the human connection with the planetary consciousness whilst at the same time gradually undergoing their own "angelic" integration.

These so-called primitive peoples are the ones who have worked directly with the planet and have helped to maintain its integrity whilst the excessive and thoughtless acts of the, inaptly named, developed world has brought the planet perilously close to destruction.

Nine thousand years ago humans and angels made their final integration within the thirteen groups. Further refinements were made to the physical body, all be it very subtle ones, and, for the first time, the final versions of man and woman stood firmly on the planet.

Everything changed.

All areas of life were affected and everything that lived on the planet also changed. The energies of life hit a high point and all forms of life flourished.

The taking on of a physical body, by the six higher civilisations, altered their perceptions of life and their role within it. The first major change was to their diet. Up until now their main source of "food" had been the planet's own energy, supplemented by nuts and fruits. Now, with their increased physical density, heavier, denser food was needed. They began with fruits and nuts but quickly added grains and pulses and, finally, were forced to add heavy protein in the form of meat.

Their consciousness levels were very much higher than that of the primate-humans and were, therefore, able to make much more efficient use of the resources around them. Farming and cultivation became much more widespread, bringing their food much closer to home than had been the case of their hunter-gatherer predecessors. Their approach to hunting was also a little more enlightened. In order to make use of the animals around them for food, they would enter into the mass consciousness of the animal group, they were about to hunt, and ask permission to take and use a defined number, as their needs dictated, and then take the animals that they needed and no more.

All of the different elements involved in this process were happy to allow this form of hunting. Only the animals required were taken and they were treated with full respect for their sacrifice. It was a case of literally asking the animal for its permission to take its life and make use of its body, a requirement, and a respect, that we have totally forgotten.

Gradually, by working with particular groups of animals that provided the greatest amount of benefit, several species were domesticated. This domestication process had already been begun some time earlier, but it was now begun in earnest and with definite purpose.

Again, nothing was done to cause these animals any kind of distress. As far as was possible, these animals were given the choice, through their own and the planet's mass consciousness, as to whether they wished to take these steps or not. There was always freedom of choice and respect.

Larger settlements were set up to bring large groups of people together and the building of permanent structures was begun. Up until now, the primate-humans had lived in temporary living accommodation in the form of huts and caves. By domesticating animals and developing crop farming methods, it was possible to bring a large number of people together and the foundation for civilisations were laid.

Everyone was very happy, they had an abundant supply of food and other necessities, they continued to interact with the planet, its life and energies. Life was new and exciting and constantly changing as new areas of potential were investigated and made use of. A physical paradise now existed where all could live in harmony and everyone's needs were simply and easily met.

It was now that the problems began.

The energy emissions of the planet, troublesome in the past, now played their final trick and put a final twist into the human saga which is only now, at the end of the twentieth century, finally being unravelled.

All of the life, that exists throughout the whole of Creation, is comprised of energy. This energy, soul, consciousness, life force, etc. etc., builds around itself a physical form which represents its essence, its level of being. Human life has adopted the densest level of body form throughout the universe, this is what makes us totally unique. Adopting this level of existence has had a considerable affect upon the level of being that we actually are.

In order to exist on Earth, we have had to adapt ourselves to the planet's own energy structures. The planet's energy levels were adopted in order to generate and nurture Earth's considerable diversity of life forms as physical entities in their own right. These life forms have a level of awareness, consciousness, that is suitable for their existence which also encompasses frequencies of energy that reflect that level of being. Higher forms of life, as represented by us, have a different level of awareness that is reflected in the range of energy frequencies that we are essentially comprised of.

The planet emits an energy "signature" that resonates at seven point five six cycles per second. This frequency corresponds very closely to the energy "signatures" of the life that it generated. In order to become physical, the angels needed to modify their own energy "signature" to encompass this frequency. By taking on this frequency, it meant that all of the other frequencies, of which they are comprised, began to be slowed and slowing down frequencies of consciousness reduces that soul's abilities to exist at its original level of awareness.

The planet actually emits a huge range of energy frequencies that span many dimensions, however, in order to exist as a physical body, that body's base frequency has to correspond to this energy level. This is why, traditionally, the energy of the human base, or root, chakra has resonated at seven point five six cycles per second (7.56Hz).

Bearing in mind that the lowest end of the frequency range, contained within the consciousness of our angel origins, is seventy five thousand cycles per second, this involved a considerable drop in energies.

The full depth and implications of these difficulties now began to be fully realised and gradually accepted by our ancestors. A way needed to be found to work within these lower frequencies, in order to fulfil "The Human Plan", whilst maintaining as high a level of consciousness as possible.

What was eventually decided was to divide the human consciousness into two parts. One part would live out a physical life, whilst the other part, the "Higher Self", would remain out of the body. The "Higher Self" would assist the "Physical Self" in learning as much as possible about human existence whilst undergoing a sequence of planned life times.

This learning process would ultimately lead to the two elements of the self being re-united into one "complete" being, thereby achieving the goals of "The Human Plan".

This is the underlying thinking behind the "Karmic Cycle" and this is the process we began to explore seven thousand years ago.

The rest, as they say, is history. Until now.

We have finally arrived at the point where we can begin the process of consciousness integration.

The process of karma has been an interesting journey. A journey full of adventure, joy and, sometimes, a degree of suffering. It has been a learning process on a grand scale and one which has been very successful. We now understand the planet, and its energies, the human body, and its energies, and have discovered a way in which the two can exist comfortably together without conflict.

Karma finished, by common consent, with the closing of 1996. This has freed up humanity to move onwards and to take on the energies contained within the Higher Self. The final decision to proceed with the integration process was made on the 6th of August 1997.

The human condition has always incorporated a very large range of energy frequencies which have been represented by the thirteen chakras, seven chakras within the body and six chakras that linked the crown to the Higher Self.

The integration process is achieved by the six higher, non physical, chakras overlying the six lower, physical, chakras and the energies, of the six higher chakras, being slowly drawn into the body. This is having an enormous affect on our bodies and our energies and will be discussed further in the next chapter. The whole of the integration process should be complete by the end of the year 2000 and our final transition, into full consciousness, should be complete by 2011.

Chapter Five

The Higher Self

To understand that which we have come to call "The Higher Self", we must first begin to understand the true nature of energy.

Scientifically, we define energy as the capacity to perform defined pieces of work, such as moving an object. Medically, we define energy as our ability to get out of bed in the morning and perform daily tasks. These definitions describe purely mechanical forms of energy.

Energy is really the building block of everything of which we, the planet, and all of its life, the stars and the universe are ultimately comprised. We exist in a space which we see as being defined by three dimensions. These dimensions give us our physical parameters, length, height and depth. Time is beginning to be seen as the fourth dimension but, in scientific terms, we are having difficulty getting our collective heads around the implications of this concept.

The truth is slowly beginning to emerge through the realms of quantum physics and advanced theoretical mathematics.

In terms of quantum physics, we exist because something, somewhere, thinks we exist. Mathematically (using the definitions implied through the theory of the mathematics found in revolving spheres), all life exists because it encompasses a very large number of dimensions and, for example, human life is a reflection of activity on these other dimensions. The mathematical definition is the place where we shall begin our investigations.

Our world is a strange place. Nowhere else, within the whole of Creation, does a comparative world exist (actually, there is one, but it is not yet ready to be inhabited). We are literally, in our human form, the densest form of life throughout this universe. But, at the same time, we are so much more than just physical tissue.

We are a soul. A created consciousness.

We exist, as physical beings, because we chose to explore the possibilities presented by an available opportunity. The reality is that we are not physical at all, but are comprised of a multi-dimensional being which has existed in many places and in many forms.

In our true state we are a huge quantity of energy which can choose to exist on many levels and in many different forms. The only limit to our potential is our imaginations. Life exists in many variations on many worlds throughout our universe and all of these worlds are accessible to us. We are "Angels". This is our true form and our true origins. We were created in order to explore, on behalf of the Creator, all that this universe has to offer.

So, what is energy?

Energy is that which is required in order to exist, it is the "stuff" that allows for that potential to be realised. It is the fields of possibility made reality. We actually have very few words within our vocabulary which can be used to describe a pure form of energy. The term energy is usually defined by the "type" of energy that is being described eg. electrical energy, mechanical energy, chemical energy etc. and therefore trying to find suitable words to explain what is meant by "pure" energy, that is energy that exists in a form that is not manufactured by another process, is extremely difficult.

The only quantifiable definition that we have is to look at this pure form of energy in terms of its "dimensions".

We see ourselves as inhabiting a world that is defined by three dimensions; length, depth and height. These can only describe our physical world and our actual location within it. When it comes to defining the space we occupy in terms of consciousness, these words are woefully inadequate.

The word "dimension" also has another definition and that is: a defining band of energy which encompasses the energy potential which exists between one defining band and the next. In this sense a dimension is a band of energy of a particular frequency. These defining bands are stacked one upon another in an ascending "stack" with the lowest energy frequencies at the bottom. Our three dimensions are the lowest three bands of the stack.

Some of the scientists from the American Space Agency, NASA, began to look at the way in which the forces, which are inherent in all massive objects, such as planets, actually work. These investigations brought about a new branch of mathematics which they have called "The Mathematics of a Revolving Sphere". In all scientific studies of moving objects the way in which the forces acting upon that object are investigated is to freeze the object in time and space and to work out the forces whilst the object is "frozen". This "frozen" situation never actually exists in real life. What the NASA scientists set about doing is to calculate these forces whilst the object is still moving.

Initially, they had extreme difficulty in making any headway into their mathematical proofs until they hit on the idea of adding dimensions beyond the accepted three.

Once they did this, all of their theories and proofs began to fall into place. So far, their mathematical proofs "prove" the existence of over thirty dimensions with the implication that there are many more beyond this number.

The outcome of their theories is that they say that in order for us, humans, to exist in our three dimensional world we have to exist in a space that encompasses many more dimensions and our activities, on Earth, are a reflection, a shadowing, of events which first take place across these other dimensions.

For the first time, with these mathematics, we have a "scientific" basis for a definition of consciousness.

As stated previously, our total consciousness is a vast quantity of energy. By using our definition of dimensions, backed up by the mathematical proof, we can now give some idea of the vastness of that energy and the real size of us.

We also have to become slightly technical in our definition. The standard method of measuring energy frequency is to use cycles per second. This is also known as Hertz, where one Hertz is one cycle per second. What is meant by one cycle per second is that most forms of energy have the shape of a wave. This occurs because the energy, in order to maintain a balance within itself, incorporates both a positive and a negative component. As the "packet" of energy moves through space and time it has to switch between positive and negative charges creating a wave like, cyclic, movement. A complete cycle is where the value of the wave, travelling in its positive direction, begins at zero. It travels, in a constant curve, up to its maximum position and then follows a constant curve back to zero. It then reverses the whole process in its "negative" direction. One cycle is, therefore, the energy "packet" travelling from zero to its maximum in the positive, returning to zero and travelling to its maximum in the negative, and returning to zero. For example, the station settings on your radio are measured in Hertz, these are cycles per second for radio waves.

So, as far as the human consciousness is concerned, shall we start at the bottom.

The root chakra, the energy that literally "roots" us onto the planet, encompasses our "normal" three dimensions. This is a frequency range of 7.56Hz to, approximately, 7,500 Hz. The second chakra has a frequency range of 7,500 Hz to 12,000 Hz and adds one more dimension. The third's range is 12,000 Hz to 25,000 Hz and adds another dimension, the fourth adds two dimensions and ranges from 25,000 Hz to 40,000 Hz. The fourth, or heart, chakra is an interesting one as it is the meeting point for the "lower", physical body energies and the "higher" spiritual energies. The fifth's range is 40,000 Hz to 50,000Hz and adds a further dimension. The sixth's is 50,000 Hz to 60,000 Hz adding a further two dimensions and, finally, the crown's range is 60,000 to 75,000 Hz and adds three dimensions, bringing the total number of dimensions up to thirteen.

The range of energies from the crown to the Higher Self ranges from 75,000 Hz for the eighth chakra to up to 250,000 Hz for the thirteenth. The total dimensional spread for these chakras goes from fourteen up to at least twenty nine and, with some people, as high as forty three.

All of the frequency values are approximate as they will vary from individual to individual, but it should be sufficient to give you some idea of the frequency range contained within the human body.

This all begins to sound a little strange. The frequency range is fine, although the idea may be new to most people, but to suggest that we can accommodate more than three dimensions within the physical body is probably beginning to sound a little far fetched.

To understand this concept, we have to look at the functions of the chakras, in relation to the physical body, but especially to the role of the root chakra.

Each chakra represents an element of our total consciousness and relates to our physical personality. Each chakra links into, and interacts with very specific regions and organs within the physical body. However, it is the root chakra which gives form and structure to the body itself.

The reason why the root chakra is so named is because it does literally "root" us into the physical realms and although this chakra has its link to specific organs, its main role is to provide the whole of the body's physical structures. In other words, everything physical is provided by the root chakra. Although the other chakras relate very specifically to organs within the body, and influence the functions of those organs, they are not responsible for constructing those organs. Therefore, the only chakra which is concerned with the actual construction of the body is the root and this is why it contains the three "physical" dimensions.

If we can accept the definition of dimensions, a defining band of energy which encompasses a particular range of energy frequencies, then it becomes much easier to understand the concept that the human chakras are able to incorporate more than three dimensions within the confines of the physical structure and still remain physical. For those to whom the idea that the chakras relate to elements of personality and to specific bodily organs is new, a brief list is set out below.*

The root chakra is located at the very base of the coccyx. its primary function is to root the consciousness, the soul, into the physical world. its secondary function governs our response to situations which threaten our security, the so called fight or flight response. Although it is the chakra which governs the whole of the body's physical structures, it relates specifically to the spine, the kidneys and the urinary system.

If you have health problems such as a weakness in the spine or have urinary problems, then your "security" has been undermined in some way at some time in the past.

The second chakra is located at about the point where the spine meets the pelvis. its primary function relates to the part of our consciousness which deals with our creativity. its secondary function deals with sexual relationships. It relates to the sex organs, ovaries and uterus etc. in women and the testes etc. in men.

The third chakra is located about one inch (25mm) above the tummy button. its primary function is the part of our consciousness which deals with personal power. its secondary function is to deal with the emotions. It relates directly to the liver, gall bladder, spleen, pancreas, stomach and the intestines. It also relates to some elements of the central nervous system.

The fourth chakra is located over the heart. its primary function is to connect the higher spiritual energies to the lower physical energies. its secondary function is the part of our consciousness that expresses love, be that for the self or

---

* For a fuller explanation of the chakras and how they relate to the physical body, see "The Healing Book" by Chris Thomas and Diane Baker.

for others. It relates directly to the heart, blood and the circulatory system, the endocrine system, and the immune system, particularly to the thymus gland.

The fifth chakra is located in the throat, midway between the adams apple and the chin. its primary function is the part of the consciousness which deals with self expression, in all of its many aspects. its secondary functions are communication and judgement. It relates directly to the lungs and the bronchial channels, the vocal chords and the metabolism, particularly to the thyroid gland.

The sixth chakra is located in the centre of the forehead, just above the bridge of the nose. its primary function is the part of our consciousness that deals with our spirituality. its secondary function is our psychic vision. It relates directly to the ears, nose and the left eye, the lower brain and the rest of the central nervous system. It also relates to the pituitary gland.

The seventh chakra is at the top of the head, in a direct line with the spine. its primary function is the entry point for the higher spiritual energies that link us to our Higher Self. It relates directly to the upper brain, the right eye and the pineal gland.

So, it can be seen that the chakras have a huge influence on the body's structures and organs. Illness occurs because the element of personality to which a particular organ(s) relates is not being fulfiled.

When the decision to split the self and the Higher Self into two separate but connected parts was made, the energies contained within the chakras was also suitably modified. Up until that point all efforts had been made to incorporate the full dimensional spectrum into a physical body.

This reduction in energy potential slowed down all of our mental and physical functions and we became the beings that we are now. It has only been in the last two hundred years that we have begun to realise that we do have a higher potential or indeed, a Higher Self.

The Higher Self is the rest of us, connected but also separate. It has undertaken all of the jobs that we have been unable, during our period of separation, to do. We all chose a role, within the confines of "The Human Plan", in order for physical life to be understood. Our lower selves have been far too busy with the life that it is living to put a particular lifetime into the overall context. This has been one of the roles of the Higher Self during this particular period. It has been a mix of guide, advisor, director, keeper of records, etc. helping us to fulfil our particular chosen role.

These roles are now beginning to change. The Higher Self is becoming more and more readily accessible. The higher energies, of the Higher Self, are gradually beginning to filter down into the seven lower chakras and the process of consciousness integration is well underway.

The integration process is, now, comparatively straight forward. The physical chakras, the lower seven, have always had a particular colour associated with them because of their particular frequencies. The root has been red, the second orange, the third yellow, the fourth green, the fifth blue, the sixth indigo and the crown violet.

As we undergo the integration process, these colours are changing. The consciousness integration process is undergone by the six higher chakras overlying the six lower chakras and their energies are slowly drawn into the lower chakras. This process is having an enormous affect upon the chakras' energies and on the body itself.

This integration process was begun in earnest in August 1996 with the switching on of the primary global energy centre. The switching on had three major affects. The first was to activate the new thirteen global energy centres and to activate the new global ley line grid (this will be discussed in chapter 8).

The second affect was to switch on the so called junk DNA contained within the DNA helix. The implications of this switching on are very far reaching. Our DNA is our primary memory system. Everything that we have ever been has been stored away in this memory bank. Re-activating this section of DNA allows us to clear out much of our unwanted debris, memories etc..

There has been a huge increase in the number of "odd" viruses in the past couple of years and these are directly due to this clearance. Every time that we encountered a viral infection, in all of our previous lifetimes, we stored it away for future reference. The reason for storing this kind of information is that if we neglected some part of our consciousness then we could call upon a suitable stored virus to infect a part of our bodies that related to that particular chakra forcing us to deal with the particular problem. As we have, effectively, gone beyond the point where such illnesses would be useful, we can clear out all of these stored memories. As we let go of these virulent memories, they have, sometimes, produced a mild form of infection in order to remind us that there are still some areas of our lives which require some clearance work in order to allow the integration process to proceed more smoothly.

A further element of this clearance is that as the junk DNA switches back on and our memory banks are wiped clean of unwanted rubbish, it allows other elements of our DNA to begin re-combining.

When we began our investigations into physical life, we were consciously fully integrated. This meant that all of our faculties were intact and our DNA was in its original form, that is, there were thirteen strands to the DNA helix. As we gradually lost our full potential these original patterns broke down and reduced to the usual two strands that we have today. All of the components of the missing eleven strands have been stored away within the cell structure until such time as we completed "The Human Plan". The time of completion is now and this DNA debris is gradually re-combining to return us to our former capabilities. There are many people on the planet who currently have three completed strands and some have as many as five. However, we cannot fully undergo our final transition until we have, individually, fully reconstructed seven strands.

The third affect of the global primary energy centre was to begin the energy integration process. The colours of the chakras have begun to change as they incorporate the six higher chakras.

The chakras, when they are clear and operating correctly, spin, (this is actually the meaning of the word chakra, it is Sanskrit for spinning wheel). From the side they look like a cone with its point connected to the spine, from the front they look like a spinning wheel, or as someone once described them, an extractor fan. The new chakra colours have a base colour and are "shot" through with flecks of other colours which sparkle as the chakra spins. The root changes to a copper gold with flecks of clear gold, violet and blue. The second has a base colour of a shimmering, vibrant blue with flecks of clear gold, violet and copper gold. The third is a clear, sparkling green with flecks of gold, violet and blue. The fourth's base colour is transparent with flecks of gold, it also has a collection of flecks of violet, green, blue and copper gold. The fifth, sixth and seventh have the same background colour as the fourth with the same colour flecks, the difference between them is that the number of flecks reduces as you go up to the seventh which is totally transparent.

To give some idea of the level of change that is occurring, the new chakra colours incorporate energies 10,000 times greater than the old chakra colours. This is the magnitude of our transitions.

Most people, currently, are about thirty to fifty percent through this transition process. The pace of change is set to accelerate and we should all have completed our transitions by the end of the year 2000.

The other affects of these changes has been to clear out all of the rubbish that we have been carrying around with us for a very long time. As we have lived through this current lifetime, we have tended to accumulate varying degrees of emotional detritus. These have been stored away in bodily organs causing illnesses of varying degrees of severity. As we undergo our transitions, this debris has had to be cleared. It has not been a question of it should, but must, be cleared. The body, in conjunction with the Higher Self, has made it very clear that we could no longer hang onto this unwanted rubbish. So for many, these past couple of years have been eventful, or even extremely traumatic, as we have followed our need to be clear of past problems and neglect of our core being.

In our past, if we decided to ignore the needs of our soul we could get away with it by ignoring the problem, storing the hurt away in an appropriate bodily organ and get on with our lives. Somewhere in the future we would have a major illness, or even possibly die, but we had further lifetimes to resolve these issues and, therefore, there was no great hurry to listen to the prompts of our Higher Self to sort ourselves out.

Now, the situation is very different. The further we go down the integration route, the less tolerant our bodies are of our transgressions. If we are faced with, say, an emotional problem, we have to deal with it there and then or we end up with an immediate symptom, such as pain.

There are no safe degrees of latitude any more, if we do not immediately deal with our problems, our bodies let us know very quickly and the closer to full integration we get, the faster is the body's response time. There is a price to pay, even for success.

The Higher Self has also undertaken numerous other tasks, some of which were discussed in detail in *"The Journey Home"**. Probably the most interesting tasks are the ones which we have been consciously unaware of. The task of maintaining humanity plc. has been extremely complex and very demanding. Virtually all of the necessary maintenance jobs have been carried out by our higher selves whilst we have been asleep. Maintaining humanity's place on the planet has been like any other job, there has been paperwork to do, accounts to keep, gardens to be trimmed and weeded and all the other tasks that are necessary to keep us and the planet happy.

We have had, and continue to have, full responsibility for the planet and the affect that we have on it. If we cause stresses on one side of the planet by, for example, extensive deep mining or detonating nuclear weapons, we have had to relieve these stresses by helping them to release in another part of the planet. This stress relief usually takes the form of an earthquake or a volcanic eruption. All of these stress relief works have been carried out by groups of individuals whilst their physical bodies were asleep.

---

* *The Journey Home* is by the same author and published by Capall Bann.

There have been many other jobs to do, when there have been armed conflicts or earthquakes etc., groups of people have gone out and given healing to the sick and wounded. Most of us have been largely unaware of our nocturnal journeyings, but next time you wake up in the morning feeling like you haven't slept, you'll know why.

Another example would be the new ley line grid and its' integration with the old grid. Very many people have been involved with this work for a period of over fifty years. It has been a project of immense scope and has involved a considerable amount of effort. But the work is complete and many of those involved are now ensuring that the energy flow is maintained at full strength, whilst counteracting the many strains and drains that our unknowing, physical life styles put upon it.

All of this is now rapidly changing. As we integrate more and more of our consciousness we effectively become our own Higher Selves and our view of the world and our activities upon it also changes.

We can no longer turn a blind eye to the actions of others who do not understand the consequences of their actions. Oppressive political regimes who do not serve their people are increasingly being overthrown by the people themselves, building projects which do not blend in with the landscape are actively being fought, companies which cause environmental damage are being prosecuted, and many other instances of oppression and greed are no longer tolerated. A global civil war is quietly taking place, but from the inside out.

The greater the number of individuals who let their own, inner, light shine out into the world, the fewer are the dark corners where others can hide.

The Higher Self has also taken very many decisions as to the directions in which our physical lives have taken. Sometimes we have had a feeling of being given advice or a gentle nudge and many people have attributed these to outside sources, such as "spirit guides". Not all, but most instances of this kind of inspiration and guidance has been by the Higher Self. This does not mean to say that spirit guides do not help us or is it being suggested that they do not exist, it is just that we are so used to being separated from our Higher Selves that we have assumed that any "communication", from anywhere other than our own minds, must come from a source that is external to ourselves.

There is also an element of ego involved in these situations. Most people feel that it sounds much more important to say that they communicate with spirit guides than to say that they talk to their Higher Self. The only problem with that is that if they really understood our origins then to say that you communicate with your Higher Self is actually saying that you communicate with an "Angel".

The final decision made by the Higher Self, acting on behalf of the lower self without its conscious knowledge, was taken on the night of August the 6th 1997. This decision has had, and will continue to have, very far reaching implications.

We all chose to take part in "The Human Plan". This was a choice made by each individual twenty thousand years ago. When we realised that there were problems that needed to be overcome, seven thousand years ago, we each formulated our own individual plan which was designed to add to the total sum of our knowledge about how to be physical whilst being able to incorporate our total consciousness. The process we have come to know as "Karma".

The road that each of us has travelled has not been easy. Some of the choices that we have needed to make along the way have been extremely difficult. There have been many instances where it was easier to put off a difficult decision until the next life time and just get on with enjoying the one we were living at the time.

These delaying tactics have meant that some of us have ended up with a great deal of tough decisions to make in this, our last, karmic lifetime.

There have been a number of people who were unable, for very many reasons, to make all, or even some, of those tough decisions this time around. Then there are others who have made some headway along their chosen path and there are others who have completed all of their chosen work several lifetimes ago.

Whatever state of completion an individual was in, a final decision needed to be made about each individual's involvement in the closing acts of "The Human Plan" and this was the decision made on the 6th of August.

The decision that had to be made was this: have I, as an individual, made sufficient headway along my chosen path to be able to make the final clearances necessary to be a part of the final phase of "The Human Plan"?

Nobody sat in judgement of anyone else. Each individual made their own assessment of their own state of readiness and made their own final decision based on the results of that assessment.

Freedom of choice of the individual is absolute, nobody has the right to stand in judgement of another, whatever the circumstances. Not even the Creator has that right.

This decision making process resulted in individuals who can be placed into three groups. There is one group who have worked diligently and consistently with their individual plan and have completed all of their chosen tasks. There is another group who have travelled some way through their individual plan and only require a little assistance to see them through. Then there is another group of individuals who made little or no progress along their chosen routes.

Each individual, that is every single person who chose to be a part of "The Human Plan", made their own decision, whether they are currently physical or not, and the outcome of this process is for each individual to act upon their decision in their own chosen way.

The outcome of the decision making process is this, those who have completed their chosen tasks will move onwards to complete the integration process, those who did not complete their chosen tasks but wish to take part in these completions will be assisted, as they require, to do so or, they have chosen to be a part of the completion but have chosen not to take an active role but will act as observers. The others, who decided for themselves that they were not in a state of final readiness, will move on to another world where they will be able to continue with their chosen plans until they judge themselves ready to make their own transitions.

This is where humanity is currently poised. Those who chose to complete their transitions into full consciousness are advancing along their chosen routes and are set to make the final leap when the time is finally right.

Those who felt that they required some assistance are receiving that assistance, from those who have chosen to provide it and are progressing at their own pace. Those who decided that they were not ready for their own transitions are gradually leaving the planet, in a method of their own choosing, to continue with their individual plans on a new Earth.

Humanity plc has reached its targets and produced a new prototype which is startling in its beauty and elegance. There only remains to make the final decision of when this new model goes into final production and that will also be an individual and collective decision.

Chapter Six

Other Forms of Universal Life

Having reached this point in the narrative, it should be very clear that mankind is not alone in the universe. Our uniqueness does not extend to being the limit of Creation.

We have always been aware of our origins and all of the civilisations that exist within the universe, but we have been so busy with our work to complete "The Human Plan" that we have not paid them much attention.

We have touched upon some of the work carried out by some of the other civilisations in helping us to achieve our chosen experimentations and we can now look at these races in a little more detail and how they helped or influenced our progression.

To start at the top.

The Creator is everything. All that exists has ultimately come from the Creator. Everyone of us has a different view of who or what the Creator is and, therefore, we are not about to enter the danger filled field of religion. Instead, we can look at the Creator in terms of how It functions and how life cycles are structured and the ultimate purpose of universal life.

The Creator has created all things in order to experience, to learn.

In order to create an individual soul, the Creator releases a "spark" of Itself which is imbued with the Creator's sense of curiosity and freedom of choice.

This "spark" is free to roam the universe and choose its own place within it. The Creator does not direct the actions of its sparks, but allows them to experience for itself who it is, where it is and what its limitations are. Freedom of choice is absolute and cannot be taken away from the individual nor can the choices, made by the individual spark, be judged by anyone other than the spark itself. The Creator does not judge, It only experiences.

The free will experienced within the universe allows each and every being to experience and explore as they choose. Each star, planet and being lives many lifetimes of experience on their return journey from the Creator and back to the Creator. As "life" ceases and the divine spark returns to the source, at a time when the spark chooses to return, the individual carries with them all of the experiences and memories that that soul has undergone. It is in this way that the Creator learns. As each and every consciousness ultimately returns to the Creator, and becomes one with the Creator, so the Creator's experience grows.

The creator is the sum of all experience and the sum of all consciousness. The creator is one but composed of the many. Each individual consciousness, that returns to the Creator, remains individual, but also becomes a part of the whole.

The creation of a new universe begins with the formation of the universal "envelope". This envelope defines the limits to the universe and is the vessel within which the universal energies are contained.

In order to maintain the balance of energies, the universe itself is imbued with its own spark, its own consciousness.

This universal consciousness is made up of thirteen beings who are protectors, co-ordinators, arbitrators, memory, repairers, co-creators and the many many other functions that the "management" of a universe requires.

These beings maintain the balance of the universe and all of its fluctuating energies and complexities of life forces. They hold a memory of all of the Creator's work and every action and re-action that takes place within the universe, they hold the parameters of the universe in place, add and divide all energies to maintain the universal whole.

In short, if the Thirteen Beings did not exist, neither would this universe. They were Created at the time of the universe and, when this universe ceases to exist, they will return to the Creator.

As was stated in chapter one, the first free moving, free acting inhabitants of the universe were the Six Higher Civilisations. These beings are described as "Higher" only in the sense that they are created from the highest energies of all of the free moving forms of life that inhabit the universe.

These beings were created in six different regions of the universe and each civilisation has their own characteristics and appearance. To us, they all look the same, but the differences exist in subtle variations in their energy frequencies.

The areas of the universe in which these beings originated are not visible from Earth. Our astronomical instruments are only capable of seeing regions of our own galaxy, or of other close galaxies which are not too distant from Earth. There is another reason why we cannot see their home worlds and that is to do with the distance between us in terms of energy. Even if they lived close enough to us for our telescopes to see, they would be far outside of our visible or even sensing spectrum.

Their life times span a very large number of years that usually run into the hundreds of thousands. They are the first born of the Creator and exist at a level much closer, than other life forms, to the Creator.

The sexes are not differentiated in any way as all are both male and female whilst being neither. This description would imply androgynous individuals, however, the concept of male and female does not exist and individuals do not exhibit characteristics of either male or female but just exist as individuals. This could be seen as a state of perfection as all energies are balanced.

With us for example, male energies and female energies exist in all of us, it is a self chosen imbalance in these energies that creates either male or female.

As these beings exist in a state of pure energy, without any form of physical body, they have no need for physical food but take sustenance from the worlds around them. This is a process that would be like us standing in direct sunlight and taking in nourishment directly from the sun. This means that they can be maintained by virtually any and all regions of the universe.

Travel does not have any constraints as they do not need any form of craft. They do not have a requirement to carry food nor do they require an atmosphere to breath, tools or instruments are not needed as they can carry out virtually any "work" psychically. They communicate telepathically and can span the whole of the universe with this type of communication.

These beings travel frequently to Earth to assist us in our work. These visits are currently increasing as we approach the time when our transitions can begin. Many people are aware of these beings and a number of mediums have begun to work with them. There are also a growing number of reported sightings but because most of these are by astronomers and astronauts they are not widely discussed. There have also been direct sightings on the planet at several times in the past. Unfortunately, these sightings have tended to produce new religions where these "Angels" are worshipped.

All of us, who have been involved in "The Human Plan" are of these beings. This is the origin of the human race. When we speak of Heaven, this is where we mean, the realms of the Six Higher Civilisations, a life of near perfection, as "Angels", close to the Creator.

With the successful integration of the Six Higher Civilisations, into the universal void, came the desire to investigate a more "physical" form of existence. The Six Higher Civilisations were considered to be too close to the Creator and their perceptions judged too close to its for there to be enough scope for new experience. Other forms of life were to be created that could perceive the universe from a different perspective. For these forms of life, seven very different regions of the universe were chosen. These are seven very distinct forms of life which differ from each other in very marked ways, with each being perfectly adapted to the environment of their home worlds.

These seven, physical, life forms have been in existence for four and a half million years, each developing and progressing in their own way and at their own pace.

The Six Higher Civilisations have assisted and advised them, in their evolution, in ways which have been appropriate to each group. This advice has been freely given and in ways which each of the Seven Lower Civilisations requested. Their freedom of choice has always been maintained.

In the same way as we have had opportunities for change and progression, each of these seven groups have had similar opportunities.

In order for each life form to return to the Creator, they must be able to raise their own energy frequencies close to that of the Six Higher Civilisations. The only way to achieve this is to choose to take the opportunity for change as their particular section of the universe passes through areas of energy similar to that where Earth is currently positioned. Like the choices we currently face, the majority of individuals must be ready to make a change and consciously want for a change to occur.

Of the seven, two have already began to make the shift away from a physical structure into a more pure energy form and a third is close to being able to make this leap.

The remaining four exist at quite different levels of development, varying from remaining in their, virtually, original form to approximately half way along their path of evolutionary potential.

The first of these groups, to have made their transition, are centred around the Pleiades, the second are located around a star system we identify as NGC 584 and the third are the life forms associated with Sirius.

The four other groups exist in areas of the universe which are, so far, uncharted by us.

The Pleiadeans are a very interesting race of beings who, more than any other in this universe, most closely resemble human appearance and physiology.

They were the first of the seven groups who began to understand the Creator's purpose and motives. They welcomed close co-operation with the Six Higher Civilisations and have striven to make the change, from their original level of existence to that of the Six Higher Civilisations, with open and abundant enthusiasm.

They have also been prepared to help others along on their own evolutionary path with great love and understanding. The Pleiadeans have assisted us many times and continue to do so during the current transitional phase.

The Pleiadeans tend to be about 1.8m (6ft) in height and adopt the appearance of being either male or female. This gender expression is not strictly necessary as they are all close to an androgynous energy balance. They appear to be human but have an inner "glow" and an energy that makes them appear slightly less than solid. As they have not yet completed their transition to a "full" energy form, they still require to use vehicles for inter-stellar travel. These craft take the form most of us think of as flying saucers. This is not the only shape of craft that they use, but it is the one with which most of us will identify.

Their current role, as far as we are concerned, is to use their craft as "transformer" stations to help step down the frequency of energies to a level that we can easily accept. As our abilities to assimilate higher frequencies of energy increase, the number of these transformer stations is rapidly reducing.

Unless deliberately made visible, these craft are invisible to our detection devices. This does not mean that they are deliberately hiding, it is just that their materials technology began from a different root to ours and we cannot detect the materials that their craft are made from. Neither can we detect their communications as they use a form of thought waves that can be transmitted over distances of several hundred light years and do not involve any form of measurable wave.

The Pleiadeans have used this form of communication to contact a number of individuals on Earth. These communications have been useful in helping us to understand the current situation and some of the choices that we have had to make, however, it should be noted that the Pleiadeans do not have full access to all of the information relating to us and our potential future. This does not mean that what they have said is necessarily wrong, but that the information has sometimes been of potential situations which have either not been feasible or not entirely possible, however, they have acted out of a genuine concern for mankind and their messages have reflected that concern.

The Pleiadeans' home world, and the other worlds which they inhabit, have an atmosphere based upon a gas similar to carbon dioxide, but also contains a low oxygen content. They are able to breath our atmosphere by altering their internal chemistry to accommodate our higher oxygen levels but they cannot maintain this process for long periods.

They do not require to eat solid foods any longer, although what they took for food we would not consider very appetising as it consisted of a form of mud and algae, but now consume a form of energy that is a by product of their form of nuclear energy production.

All Pleiadeans are fully aware of the opportunity for change that their race faces and are making every preparation to ensure that their chance for change is not missed. They are now ready to move on to a level of existence closer to that of the Six Higher Civilisations.

The life forms from the star system we know as NGC 584 are in the process of undergoing a similar change to that of the Pleiadeans, although their evolutionary route has been very different.

Their physical characteristics are, to put it mildly, a little different to ours. To our minds a description of characters who are 0.9m (2ft 6") tall with a skin texture and colour of blue/grey leather sounds more like a character from a child's fairy tale than the highly evolved beings that they actually are. They have very large eyes and do not have a discernable nose or mouth. Their body shape is similar to that of a new born child, short arms and legs, a rounded body and a large head that appears out of proportion with the rest of their bodies. The enlarged head allows for a highly developed brain structure and their higher brain functions are exceptionally highly developed.

Ever since the first seedings of higher life forms onto Earth, those from NGC 584 have been associated with us. They were the ones who established Lemuria and were the ones who determined whether the planet was ready for those seedings. They have assisted the Six Higher Civilisations with many aspects of human development and they introduced many of our animal species to the planet.

Their home world is effectively a ball of ice that has a surface temperature that can go below 50 degrees Kelvin (about minus two hundred degrees Centigrade) in their winter time. These life forms are perfectly adapted to their world as are the plant and the few animals that share it.

They have always been very willing and able to assist us even though they found our ice ages far too hot.

These life forms are master geneticists and hold genetic records and models for all of the life throughout the universe. Most forms of life would freeze solid on their world and this makes it perfect for storing genetic material. In this task they assist the Six Higher Civilisations to record and sample endangered species or species that exist on one world and would be suitable for others.

The NGC 584 home world's atmosphere is composed of a gas similar in chemical construction to sulphur. Sulphur is also the basic building block for these beings, in the same sense as carbon is our building block. They also communicate by telepathy.

They do still travel by physical craft which tend to be cigar like in shape but they rarely enter our atmosphere. They are also ready to assist us if we choose to fully grasp our current opportunities.

The third group of physical beings, who are approaching their final stages of physical life, are those that originate in an area of the galaxy that we call Sirius.

The Sirians are about 1.4m (4ft 6") in height and are close to being a pygmy version of us. They do not have any hair and have large eyes, they are also pale skinned that has a slightly green cast.

The atmosphere of their home world is composed of gases that do not exist on Earth and would be highly toxic to us as is our atmosphere to them. It is mainly for this reason that they have not been directly involved in human development, however, some of their genetic material has been used in developing human physical DNA and this is why we have distant memories of a connection to Sirius.

Despite the atmospheric problems, they visited us on several occasions, mainly in the past. Their craft are spherical in shape with a slight elongation on the lower end. When these craft enter our atmosphere they tend to glow brightly in changing colours. These are not energy emissions but an effect similar to oxidization as the materials that comprise these craft find our atmosphere highly corrosive.

The Sirians are not directly involved in our current transition but are providing assistance to the Pleiadeans with energy manipulation techniques.

They breath by a process similar to osmosis. The area of their faces that would correspond to our noses is comprised of a thin filtering membrane that extracts out any atmospheric impurities allowing them to breath a virtually pure form of the gas they require. They have never eaten solid food but take nourishment from their atmosphere and crystal energy sources, which they manufacture and tune for this purpose. Their form of communication is by thought wave that can be powerful enough to span several galaxies.

These life forms are fully aware of their potential for change and are putting all of their efforts into making their transition as smooth as possible.

These three life forms are the ones that have completed a major step on their evolutionary ladder. Their progress has been very rapid and they are now, almost, ready to establish a new level of existence within the universe. This new level is a breathing space on the bridge between physical life and the Creator. This does not mean that they will cease their efforts to assist all life forms but they will progress onwards to higher and greater achievements.

There are four other groups of higher life forms that exist throughout the universe. These are not yet ready to fulfil their potential as they have, generally, chosen not to take full advantage of their evolutionary opportunities.

All seven of the Lower Civilisations were created at the same time and given a similar level of encouragement. The three detailed above have welcomed this encouragement and co-operation and have evolved rapidly, the remaining four have evolved, but to varying degrees and accepted varying levels of assistance.

All four life forms exist in areas of the universe too remote for our observation and, therefore, do not have have names that we can identify with.

The first, and what could be described as the least evolved, live on a planet in an area of the universe furthest away from our galaxy. These life forms are comprised mainly of a silica like material that gives them a form more resembling rock formations and rock glaciers than free moving individuals.

These life forms have retained most of their higher brain functions, but the comparatively slow pace of their lives means that they are largely incapable of perceiving life in freely moving forms.

Despite many visits from all of the other twelve civilisations, they have chosen to remain at their present pace of evolution and not change too rapidly. It is estimated that these life forms will take another 20 - 30 million years to evolve to a state where they will be able to join with the Six Higher Civilisations.

To us, this appears to be an incredibly long period of time, but in terms of how the universal time is measured, this is not really very long.

To some, the attitude of these life forms might appear to be a waste of creation, but this is not the case. These life forms recognise, within themselves, that part which is of the Creator and, therefore, fully appreciate their existence.
They are content just to be.

Two of the three remaining life forms could be taken together. Although they both have very different physical characteristics, they display very similar character traits.

It is primarily these three life forms that are responsible for the vast majority of UFO sightings, visitations and non-terrestrial phenomena on the planet.

The first group is about 1.1m (3ft 6") tall with slender bodies with, comparatively, very large heads which contain very large, black, eyes, with ears, nose and mouths that are not very prominently defined. They are silvery grey/white in colour and tend not to wear any clothing. Their physiology is closer to that of reptiles than to humans. It was their physiological structures that were the model for the first dinosaurs. These beings frequently visit Earth and are what the UFO watchers tend to call the "Greys". The craft that they travel in are very similar to those used by the Pleiadeans, that is, flying saucers.

They have developed a verbal form of language, from their early evolutionary years, but they sound more like whistles and clicks to our ears than what we would recognise as language. Their more usual, main, form of communication is by thought wave. They do eat solid food occasionally, but their main source of nourishment is energy transmissions taken from a variety of sources.

Their actions can be likened to the behaviour of some teenagers, they have a certain amount of knowledge but do not fully understand the consequences of their actions.

The second group behave in similar ways to the greys. This group varies in height, but are usually no more than 1m (3ft) tall. They are fairly round in shape, with short legs. Their heads and bodies are covered in short, dark blue hair.UFO watchers have christened these the "Blues".

This group use two forms of craft, the first is triangular in shape with two sides of the triangle being much longer than the base side. The sides of these craft are vertical, the overall appearance being like a piece of brie cheese. The second craft that they use is circular with a rounded top and bottom.

These second craft are very interesting. Inside the outer, hard, shell is a very soft interior. This soft material is, in fact, living. When the blues travel across the galaxy, they step into the living material which envelopes them and provides all life support systems whilst in flight. The craft is then flown by thought controls.

The blues and greys very often travel together as they have a common interest in humans. These two groups of beings are the ones responsible for abduction and experimentation stories. To a certain extent, many of these stories are true. Both of these races are extremely "jealous" of the human body and have been trying to develop one which they can inhabit. This does not mean that they are body snatchers. The blues have developed a very keen interest in genetics and they have been, literally, trying to build a human body for themselves so that they could transfer their consciousnesses from their own bodies into a more human form. The fact that body form follows the form of the consciousness, via the mass consciousness energy template discussed earlier, seems to have escaped their attention until very recently. They have stopped their experimentation and now only visit the planet to observe the changes that we are going through.

They do still visit their ground bases in America, however, which is where most of that country's military technological advances stem from.

The third group are comparative newcomers to our region of the universe. These beings are fairly new to inter-galactic travel and have only begun exploring areas beyond their own galaxy in the last few decades.

These beings are approximately 2.5m (8ft) tall and usually wear full environment suits that look like blue metal foil. They have large, heavy bodies with small heads, but are humanoid in shape. The reason for the small head is that it only contains sense organs, their brains are very large and are located in their chest region. Their visits are not very frequent and they tend to leave very quickly as they find the energies of the planet uncomfortable, especially all of the various noises that we constantly make. These beings are generally very peaceable and are beginning to work more closely with the Six Higher Civilisations.

From these brief descriptions, of the higher life forms throughout the universe, the universe will probably appear to be a very empty place.

Most of the Seven Lower Civilisations have spread out over several galaxies, wherever there have been planets compatible with their physiologies, and the Six Higher Civilisations exist in all areas.

There are also a huge number of planets which support an amazing range of life forms. Some of these have come from the Creator, as It is always curious, and many have come from the planetary consciousness concerned. They have not been included here as they do not have any bearing on our history or our development.

However, there is one other life form with which we share our solar system. These inhabit one of the moons of Jupiter known as Gannymede.

This moon has a surface of a mixture of liquid oxygen and hydrogen, the top two miles of which are frozen.

These life forms are an adaption of the original inhabitants of Venus who are a form of reptile fish which lived in Venus' seas and forests. These beings were adapted to live under Gannymede's icy surface. The surface is not totally frozen as there are still many active volcanoes on Gannymede.

These beings are highly intelligent and are aware of humanity's existence. They are waiting for us to contact them before they make themselves known to us as they fear our vast number of energy emanations that leave the planet in the form of radio and TV transmissions (we are far too noisy for them). They have not had any bearing on our existence.

As a further note about our constant interest in the stars. We have always been drawn to the constellation of Orion. Many of our tribal peoples have made quite a fuss about this star system. All ancient peoples have built temples to it or have made references to it in their mythologies and traditions.

Orion is a dimensional gateway of enormous significance. In order to enter or leave our solar system, travel has to be through this region of space. This is where the energy dimensions of space are condensed down to our dense level.

In order for Earth to exist, time and space had to be distorted to make it slow and dense enough for our energy capabilities. As an example of this slowing down we can use the speed of light. Light, in our region of space, travels at 186,000 miles per second.

Outside of the Orion "gate" light travels at different speeds. In the regions of the Seven Lower Civilisations, for example, it travels at between 570,000 and 1,000,000 miles per second, depending upon which part of space you are in. In the realms of the Six Higher Civilisations, light travels at speeds close to infinity.

Another example would be the energy dimensions. In our solar system, we have the three dimensions of the physical world and the sixty, or so, dimensions that "physical" consciousness occupies. As we leave our solar system, there is an increase in energy potential. Our section of the galaxy is enclosed within an energy "envelope" which has a shape similar to a rugby ball. This envelope is comprised of an energy of 738 dimensions. This is the maximum energy potential available to us until we make our full transitions.

Once we clear the Orion "gate", the energy potential explodes out to a limitless supply.

All of the journeys that we have made between our home with the Six Higher Civilisations and Earth have been made through the Orion gate and it is the memory of these travels which has given us our connections with Orion.

Chapter Seven

The Earth's Mysteries - Part One

There are many enigmas located over the whole of the planet's surface. We usually refer to these enigmas as "Sacred Sites".

All of these sites are constructed around points of highly focused energy. What must be remembered, above all else, is that everything is energy. Nothing exists without an energy to create it and nothing functions without energies of particular frequencies to provide that function.

People have always known how to use this multitude of planetary energy points but, in our headlong rush into technological answers, we have forgotten. It is only now, as our energies are changing so dramatically, that we are beginning to remember. Everything that our technology and machinery can do, we can do so much more efficiently by utilising our minds and the freely available energies.

Slowly, we are beginning to understand this fact and are starting to work with the planet and its energies and are gradually turning away from machines and the pollution and problems that they create.

As our memory gradually returns, we are awakening to the fact that all of these ancient sites had a function and we once knew how to access and utilise those functions.

Most of these ancient sites we term "sacred". This term, in itself, is totally incorrect and comes from the archeological belief that if these sites had a religious function then they must have been "sacred". In archaeology, if an ancient site is discovered where its function could not be easily determined, it was claimed that it must have had a religious function. By labelling it religious, the archaeologists could then stop thinking about it as they leave religious matters to others. Unfortunately, this meant that these sites were never investigated fully as current religions are not interested in anything that came before them or could possibly contradict their theologies. Anthropologists have largely ignored this aspect of our predecessors as they consider these people to be totally primitive and unable to comprehend "sophisticated" concepts such as those implied by modern theology.

When these sites were begun to be investigated, from a religious viewpoint, any attempt to unravel their mystery has been coloured by the imposition of our current belief systems. It has been left to those outside of the closed academic world to bring the true meanings and uses of these ancient sites to the public eye, usually to much ridicule from the scientific community. The truth is slowly emerging and is confirming much of the history discussed in the first few chapters of this book. We are so much more than we currently are and we are only now waking up to this fact.

When our planet first formed itself into a world capable of supporting life, it generated all of the energies necessary to maintain that life. As our primate ancestors developed and progressed, these energies were adjusted and finely tuned to assist in that progression.

These energies have been adjusted and enhanced ever since as our understanding, capabilities and needs have waxed and waned. The real beginnings of these energy sites is with Atlantis.

Atlantis was a place of experimentation, growth and exploration. To fuel these activities vast quantities of energy were required. The planetary consciousness could not supply these forms of energy as it would detract from its primary role of engendering and supporting all of the forms of life it was still in the process of creating and evolving.

A new form of energy was required which could "power" the work on Atlantis but did not have any adverse affects on the planet as a whole. The first of these power stations was located on part of the islands of the Azores (inevitably, the part which no longer exists). These power stations took the form of the energy generation systems which exist in the other civilisations, namely crystal energy.

Although we still work with crystals, mainly for healing purposes, and more recently to build energy enhancing matrices, our understanding of crystals cannot prepare us for the magnitude of the energy that could be generated by the ones used at Atlantis.

All of these crystals were manufactured by the inhabitants, or at least the individuals who understood the process and were able to tune the crystals very precisely to the required frequency bands. As new frequencies of energy were required, to carry out specific tasks or to support the growing population, new crystals were manufactured.

The method of manufacture was to place the palms of the hands together and to concentrate on building up an energy field of a very specific frequency. When a sufficient amount of "energy force" had been built, the hands were moved away

106

from each other, stretching the field. The ends of the fields were then sealed, mentally, and the formed energy core put into a bath of fluid. The fluid contained a wide variety of minerals and the energy "core" would attract to itself specific minerals which would enhance its specific frequencies. The energy core would be anywhere from a few centimetres long to several metres. The finished crystals would be anything up to 10m (30ft) tall and up to 4m (12ft) in diameter. These crystals could generate a huge energy field, similar in concept to an aura, and by collecting this field and running it in conduits, similar to fibre optic cables, these crystals could provide virtually limitless energy.

These were the beginnings of energy manipulation on this planet.

The dimensional gateway, which is Orion, has been mentioned previously. This gateway was, and still is, the main way in or out of our solar system. If we fired one of our rockets out into space it could travel no further than the distance to Orion. This is because our part of the galaxy is enclosed in a dimensional envelope that allows to us exist as "physical" beings. If this barrier did not exist then neither could we, at least not in our dense matter form. As our rocket would not have the capability of breaking through this dimensional envelope then it would probably spend the rest if its days sliding around the inner face of the envelope. However, if it found its way to the Orion gate then it could travel through the barrier and enter a space which exists in a different dimensional reality.

The second phase of energy development on Atlantis was the construction of a gateway similar to Orion, but on the planet itself. This gate was not strictly necessary as the travellers it was designed to accommodate could very easily travel through Orion and down to the planet. This new gate was essentially an experiment to see if such a gate could be established on the planet without blowing the planet's fuses. What this gate achieved was to allow rapid travel between the "angels" and us without having to pass through Orion. Once this gate was established, it made travel between dimensional spaces much easier and faster. It also proved that direct travel to Earth was possible and established principles and practices which were to prove useful once Atlantis had been sunk.

As Atlantis developed, new energy sources were established. These new sources served two purposes. The first was to provide sufficient power to the island itself with its growing population and energy requirements for the, by now, well established genetic research laboratories. The second reason was that the planetary consciousness had asked if its own energy resources could be enhanced.

This enhancement was achieved by creating an energy matrix linking around the whole planet. This matrix amounts to being the ley line network that has existed throughout the whole of our history and was only partially replaced with the connection and switching on of the new grid. The power "feed" for the ley grid was located in one of the new energy source locations and is now a "sacred" site.

These new power stations were located in Britain and this is why Britain was saved from the sinking of Atlantis. If Britain had been destroyed then the new ley grid would have been destroyed and could have caused untold damage on a planetary scale.

With the sinking of Atlantis and the fresh start of human life in other planetary locations, new energy structures needed to be built.

The first requirement was to maintain the ley network. This had been powered directly by crystal sources, however these would eventually run out if they were not replenished. So the first post Atlantis act was to ensure a constant, clean energy source. This was achieved by forming a new dimensional "gate" at the original supply point. This was only a one way gate, the purpose of this energy was to supply the ley grid and serves no other purpose. This gate still exists and continues to feed energy into the old grid and was the most powerful energy point on the planet until the new energy centre and grid system was switched on in August 1996.

This intake point is known as Silbury Hill in Wiltshire. The "hill" itself is a man made construction originally built about seven thousand years ago and acts as a natural accumulator, or battery.

The second energy construction, in the post Atlantis, period was the Sphinx in Egypt. This was constructed about nineteen thousand years ago and replaces the original dimensional gateway on Atlantis.

The people of this time were able to see and sense energies very easily. At Silbury, for example, the energy connected in with the planet's surface structure and created a "lightening" of the soil's structure. its visual effect was similar to a lake of water in an open field.

Egypt is a little different. At the time that the Sphinx was built, the region's climate was very different to what it is now. It had lush semi-tropical vegetation and had quite a high annual rainfall, however its underlying soil structure was mainly composed of mica. Mica is, in energy terms, a dead material. In other words, it does not allow the passage of energy through its structure. If a pan-dimensional gateway was to be constructed, then it could not be allowed to influence the planet's own energy matrices as this would go against the agreement that had been reached with the pre-human groups.

Potentially, an energy shift of this magnitude could affect the whole of the planet's underlying energy structures which could create change within the DNA structures of the pre-human population. Therefore, an energetically "dead" region needed to be found where this gateway could be located.

To avoid potential accidents, a marker was used to surround the gate to warn people that the gate existed in that location. The gateway "door" was located in a chamber below ground and under the Sphinx.

The original face of the Sphinx matched that of the body, that is, a lion. The image was changed to that of a human by a later Pharaoh.

It was anticipated that the lion image would deter the pre-human population sufficiently to prevent them from falling into the gate, it is as simple as that.

The chamber, beneath the Sphinx, still exists, although the gate has not been in use for many thousands of years. Several ancient traditions hold that the chamber was used as a store house for many of the records of Atlantis. The chamber was discovered in 1996 and excavated in 1997. At the time of writing, no information has been officially released about the contents of this chamber.

As a second phase of this type of development and constructed form of gate, another type of structure was built in South America. This was a pyramid shape built out of a type of stone that contained very high levels of quartz. The floor of the pyramid was lined with mica to prevent any potential energy leakages into the ground, keeping this structure and its energies totally insulated from the Earth's energy ley grid. Again, this gateway at Teotehuacan in Mexico has not been used for many centuries but it does still retain its capabilities and potential.

110

As we became more and more a part of the planet, we began to take a greater interest in the way in which the planet was influenced by our planetary neighbours. Up until this point we had considered ourselves to be of the universe as a whole and had not paid a great deal of attention to the solar system and the way in which it exerted influences on the Earth.

Earth is not a planet in isolation. It is influenced by the other planets and what remains of their consciousness. It is also influenced, in a very major way, by the solar system consciousness as represented by the sun. The sun is able to influence the planet in very many ways. It provides heat and light to sustain and feed the planetary life. It can also be quite destructive in its periodic shifting of its magnetic flux.

When we first began "The Human Plan" we were in full control of all of our mental and psychic faculties and we could follow the movements and note the influences of all of the solar system planets, and more distant galaxies, without the aid of any mechanical assistance.

As we began our slow, but persistent, slide into the depths of our humanness, we began to require memory "joggers" to help us remember certain pieces of information.

There are very many energy sites around the world which all have their individual "character" and connection to planetary or star system energies. For example, The Sphinx, Stonehenge and Teotehuacan all connect into the Orion Gate. In order to remember the sequence of cycles and energy connections, standing stones, or other more complex structures, were added which acted as "memory banks". Standing stones or designated "temples", the type of structure largely depended upon the choices of the particular peoples, hold the memory within the body of the stone itself. If you dowse standing stones or temples you will find that they all contain bands of energy and it is within these energy bands that the memories are stored. If you connect with these structures, by meditation or psychometry, then the stored memories can be accessed. It does need a little practice to understand what it is you are accessing, but the stones have not forgotten.

All over the planet these structures were added during a period when we were beginning our transitions from full consciousness, from 15,000 to 7,000 years ago. Other stones have been added to various sites in the intervening centuries for a large variety of purposes, but the original meanings for these structures remains intact.

All of these stones and structures, constructed during this period, were placed using the same methods. Stonehenge, The Pyramids, etc. were all constructed using a form of telekinesis. If a group of like minded individuals came together with the purpose of transporting or placing these stones then, by all concentrating their minds on the task, any object can be levitated and "flown" to its chosen location. Once in place, its energies can be imprinted with any information, using the same collective process, and read by anyone who has the knowledge to do so. This accessing of information in this way began our traditions of initiates to certain "secret" information and ultimately led to the setting up of formal religions.

What must be remembered about all of these sites, worldwide, is that they were set up for very specific purposes. There was no mystery about them, all understood their functions. There was no sense of worship, that is a very much later concept, nor was there any sense of sacredness. If an individual knew how to access the memories contained within the stones then they were free to access them. Secrets, sacredness, religions, worship and all of this type of concept only began about 5,000 years ago when we were well into our karmic existence and very far down the slide from full consciousness.

All of these stones and structures had only one purpose, to concentrate the minds and energies of those who sought out the information contained within them and reminded the searcher of the energy connections contained within the particular structure.

Most of these structures had specific energies that related to specific roles and functions. Silbury Hill was the primary energy intake point for global energies which came from a source outside of the Orion Gate. Stonehenge was a direct dimensional link to the regions beyond the Orion Gate, as was Teotehuacan and The Sphinx.

West Kennet Long Barrow was, and still is, the site of the most powerful upwelling of planetary energies anywhere on the planet. It is located directly opposite Silbury Hill so that the connections between "universal" energies and "earth" energies is as direct as possible. The long barrow was added at a much later date, about 4,000 years ago by a local chieftain who wished to be buried within the energy upwelling. Stonehenge and Silbury Hill are linked only in the sense that they share similar ranges of multi-dimensional energies. Their main differences lie in their function. Stonehenge was a two way gate, and thanks to the efforts of many individuals and groups over the past few years, it soon will be again. Silbury Hill's energies travel one way only.

Closely linked in with the Silbury Hill/ West Kennet/ Stonehenge energy link is the collection of stone circles at Avebury. Avebury served a totally different, but linked, purpose. There were originally six stone circles at Avebury linked by stone avenues, all of which contained particular ranges of information that eventually allowed the usage of Stonehenge to be re-discovered.

The idea was that you followed a sequential route, beginning at Silbury Hill. The "initiate" was "bathed" in the Silbury energies to raise their personal energy levels. As they progressed along each stone avenue and circle in sequence they collected the memories programmed into the stones, by the time they arrived at Stonehenge they had a working knowledge of the gateway.

Similar "routes" were marked out for "initiates" at all of the similar gateways located in other countries.

Stonehenge also had a second purpose. Several of the stone circles and pyramids are energetically linked around the planet and acted as planetary gateways. If you knew how to access the correct energies then you could enter a gateway, say in Scotland, and exit a corresponding gateway in, say, South America.

These gateways are a later addition to the original grid. They were only added as our higher capabilities began to be lost. As we slowed down, we required a greater number of these memory sites and energy gates which allowed for easy and rapid travel to all of the continents. Don't forget, in our original state we did not need any form of gateway, but could freely travel about the planet by means of translocation.

In Britain, because of its connections with the Atlantis energy grid, the available energies were, to all intents and purposes, limitless. In other countries, the energy supply was not quite so readily available.

The problems, or benefits, of the soil in Egypt has been mentioned above. This insulating property meant that the later Egyptian gate had to be constructed above the ground and the energy focused by linking several energy accumulating structures together.

This is the purpose of the pyramids. If you look at a map of Egypt you will see that the main pyramids form a pattern that link into the pyramids at Giza. The plan shape presented by the network of pyramids is a reflection of the stars of Orion with the Nile representing the Milky Way. This is why the three pyramids at Giza are not in a straight line, they form the layout of Orion's belt.

Each of these seven pyramids formed an energy accumulator. They all focused their energies into the Great Pyramid in the Centre of the Orion belt formation.

The shape of a pyramid tends to focus energies into its geometric centre where the energy rapidly builds up to very high levels. If you know how to tap into these energies then they can be utilised for very many purposes.

In the Egyptian pyramids, the four outer pyramids and the two smaller pyramids in the central belt, had very large crystals mounted on their outer surfaces and crystals buried within the thickness of the walls. The outside ones were located at the top, as part of the pyramidion, and on the four sides about half way down their height. These crystals were linked in to the central chamber by four crystal conduits, located in the so called ventilation or star shafts. The internally generated energy was concentrated in the central chamber, transferred through the shaft crystals to those on the outside. This energy was then collected by the pyramidion crystal and "transmitted" to the crystal on the top of the Great Pyramid pyramidion.

The energy in the central chamber of the Great pyramid was the accumulation of seven pyramids. This energy accumulation was almost equivalent to the energy available at Stonehenge.

In Palenque in South America the arrangement of their gate was a little different. The underlying geology meant that lines of energy could be drawn to a suitable point, as is the case with ley lines, and then concentrated inside a pyramid structure.

The full knowledge of the uses of all of these dimensional gates eventually became lost, however, their use did pass down into memory and this is why a number of these sites were used as a burial site by a powerful local king or chieftain. By using these gates for their burial, their soul would pass directly through the Orion gate to "Heaven".

With the sealing of these structures, following the burial, they fell into disuse and their original purpose was lost, this eventually led to the formation of other beliefs and myths about these sites.

This all begins to sound a little confusing as we have gates for one purpose and gates for another all added to the planet's surface at various times, each performing different functions and utilising different energy sources.

To sum up.

The planet has its own energies. These energies take two forms. The first is a function of the planet's construction and rotation. As the planet spins it generates a magnetic flux within its core which creates a magnet with its poles at the North and South Poles. Like all magnets, it generates lines of magnetic flux in the region between the two poles. This magnetic flux is similar to electrical impulses and can be easily measured by scientific equipment. This type of energy helps to hold the planet together in its physical form.

The second type of energy is to do with the planetary consciousness. All of the animals and plants that share our world are generated and nurtured by this consciousness. This energy field permeates the whole of the planet's structure and breaks through to the surface at numerous points. In all there are 428,384 of these points dotted all over the planet's surface with West Kennet Long Barrow being the most "powerful". Several of these points have been marked, by our ancestors, with single standing stones.

Both of these forms of "Earth Energy" are generated and maintained by the planet itself.

When we became involved with the planet, at the time of Atlantis, the planet asked that its own energies be enhanced to overcome the damage caused by the solar system changes and to assist with our work on Atlantis.

This enhancement took the form of a "grid". This is a series of ley lines laid over the whole of the planet's surface which link into and connect with the planet's own energy upwellings. The energy for this grid comes from the realms of the Six Higher Civilisations, through the Orion gate and into Silbury Hill. This first grid was established about 80,000 years ago. With the sinking of Atlantis, it was modified and put into its final form 28,000 years ago. As the old grid was being modified, six additional energy centres were added to enhance its function and correspond to the energy requirements of the soon to arrive human population. These seven energy centres have given rise to the belief that the planetary energy centres correspond to the human body's seven chakras. This is not strictly true. Although they exist on the planet, they are not of the planet but were added to enhance the work to be carried out with the new humans that arrived twenty thousand years ago.

Further modifications were made in the period 18,000 to 15,000 years ago with the addition of the gateways at the Sphinx and Teotehuacan. These were gateways to and from the planet and were deliberately insulated from the planet's energies to prevent any possible disruption to the planet's life. During the same period, Stonehenge was constructed without any form of surrounding structure or insulation. Stonehenge was the first of a new type of gateway which could interact with the planet's energies without causing disruption. This site was chosen because it was close to Silbury Hill and if anything went wrong the energies could be diverted into Silbury Hill and the already established grid. Following the successful construction and integration of Stonehenge, the other main gates were built. These are pan-dimensional gateways which are designed for travel away from the planet. As humanity began its slide into lower consciousness, a new, different type of gateway was required. These are the gates which allowed for free travel around the planet as our translocation skills began to be lost. These gates are the ones located at most of our ancient sites, stone circles, the Pyramids, etc. These gates allow travel around the planet's surface but not into space.

When the old ley grid was constructed, it contained the potential to provide sufficient energies to encompass the whole of the human consciousness. Since the start of "The Human Plan" these energies have lain dormant. About fifty years ago, work was begun on cleaning up the old grid and constructing a new grid. This new grid was required in order to provide sufficient energy to support our current change and transition. The whole of the ley grid has been modified and updated to include thirteen major energy points. There are also 43 minor energy points dotted over the Earth's surface.

The ley grid network and main energy points is usually likened to the human chakra and meridian systems. Whilst this analogy has its merits, it is not particularly accurate. The planet does not have chakras but emits consciousness energy over the whole of its surface through the 400,000 or so energy points.

The ley grid and its primary energy points were added to provide energy for humans. They do enhance and work with the planetary consciousness' energies and are built close to the planet's surface, but they were not constructed, nor are they maintained, by the planet.

Another aspect of ancient sites is the representation of animals. These representations are found all over the world and take several different forms. Some are cut into the landscape, such as the chalk carvings in Britain, some are formed by clearing areas of ground, such as the Nazca formations in Peru, and some are "mounds" built onto the landscape, such as in North America.

These representations were used in several ways.

Their original use was by tribal Shaman. All of the tribal shamanic traditions, in every part of the world, worked with the planet in ways which were appropriate to their particular location. The shaman were not only healers and mediums for people but also for the planet itself. In this sense, the animals had two purposes. Each shaman had their own "totem" animals, as indeed do every single one of us. These are animals which represent certain aspects of our personality or, in a zodiacal sense, cycles of birth. Within each tradition, each animal would represent a particular month or year.

The other, and more important purpose for these animal representations was concerned with continuity. A major role of the shaman is to work with their totem animal, or in fact all animals, to ensure their continuity within the natural whole. This has, unfortunately, been necessary as human activity has created weaknesses in the mass consciousness constructs that relate to numerous animals and plants. Where these weaknesses become extreme, the animal or plant has left the planet, in other words, become extinct.

Fortunately, there are genetic and energy records kept by those who inhabit the star system NGC 584 and it is hoped that some of these species will be reintroduced at some future date when we cease to be so careless and unthinking.

A shaman would leave his body, as in Aboriginal "dream time", and connect with the planetary mass consciousness of a particular animal group, dog consciousness, cow consciousness, snake consciousness, deer consciousness etc. and work within that consciousness to strengthen the animal group's connection to the planet and ensure the continuation of that particular species.

The work of the shaman was carried out on higher energy levels, but every one could also be a part of this type of work. By meditating on their totem animal, anyone could help maintain the animal's mass consciousness to function within the natural world. This meditation was best achieved by a walking form of meditation. This is why physical represent- ations of particular animals are represented in very large forms. In order to concentrate the mind you needed to meditate for long periods and it is easier to walk around a large path than a small path.

These meditations took place at certain times of the year but individuals were free to walk their own animals at any time they chose. Like the process of writing, walking the path of a totem animal in this way added the energy of the meditation into the ground, a form of succussing, helping to maintain the outline of the animal in the landscape and, therefore, its presence on the planet.

There were other uses for these types of meditations. The North American Indians, for example, would meditate upon a particular animal group the night before a hunt. These meditations allowed the shaman to enter the mass consciousness of a chosen animal and ask permission to kill a particular number of animals for the tribe's use. In this way, the tribe would ensure that the animals were shown full and proper respect for their sacrifice. It also meant that their hunt was more likely to be successful, however, they would ensure that they only killed as many animals as they required for their immediate needs. A very successful symbiotic relationship which honoured and respected both the animal and the tribe.

This same principal of walking meditations was also used for other purposes which did not have anything to do with animals. The fine upstanding young man at Cerne Abbas in Dorset, had two functions, one of which being connected with male fertility. If a man had fertility problems, he could carry out a meditative walk around the chalk carving and, hopefully, overcome his problem. The second reason was much more visual. The image at Cerne Abbas is designed to frighten away marauding tribesmen from other tribes. The symbol "says" there are big strong men in the vicinity and it would be unwise to mess with them, or words to that effect. Again, the energy of the symbol was imprinted into the chalk by walking meditations which involved stamping the feet of the walkers.

The act of walking these carvings wore down the vegetation, in the same way as any well walked path does, however, because they were used to imprint the energy of the meditation into the ground, it has prevented these images from becoming overgrown even though they are not usually "walked" in the same ways today.

The traditional labyrinth and spiral forms were also used for similar purposes. Instead of the meditator, or shaman, working with an animal form these constructions were used to concentrate the mind on working with the planetary consciousness. The spiral and labyrinth are a form of representation of an energy vortex. Like the bodily chakras, all energy, when allowed freedom of movement, forms itself into the shape of the vortex. When the vortex is viewed from the front or directly above, it looks like a spiral.

These forms were used for two purposes. The large spirals and labyrinths were used as walking meditations which allowed the meditator to enhance their own energies to a point where they could begin to "converse" with the planet's consciousness.

The smaller versions of these forms, such as those carved into standing stones, could be used to take an inner journey. By sitting in front of the carved representation, it was possible to use the spiral form to enter into the inner world and cleanse out any undesired character traits or just purely as a self-cleansing exercise on very deep and powerful levels.

Chapter Eight

The Earth's Mysteries - Part Two

There is another group of enigmas which has been increasing in the past few years. Since 1990, these energy forms have been growing in number and complexity. Most of these energy forms have appeared in farmers' fields but there have been a few which have fallen out of this normal pattern and have added to the mystery.

These energy forms are more usually called crop formations. There is a government censorship notice restricting the reporting of these formations which has been in place for a number of years. This is why so few of these formations are reported in the press.

In 1997, for example, there were known to be at least 100 crop formations in Britain, but no more than a dozen were reported in the press. In 1994 there were 330 known formations in Britain, the most prolific year to date and since then, whilst the actual number has been dropping, their complexity has continued to increase. Most of these complex shapes take the form of fractals and can contain several hundred circles.

These formations have a longer history than most people realise. It is assumed that they are a fairly recent phenomena but reports going back to 1654 give accounts of "mowing devils" appearing in fields. As reports of these earlier incidents were written up by the clergy, there tended to be a certain bias in their reporting. There is also an account of what appears to be a formation in the mid 1500s.

Where there has been official comment, the reason usually given is that of freak weather patterns which produce whirlwinds of ionised air. When these mini tornadoes come up against obstructions, such as hillsides, they hit the ground and form circular patterns in crops. There probably is some merit in this explanation, where the formations are of single, or short chains of circles that appear on the edges of fields. However, this model cannot fit the extremely complex, geometrically perfect formations that appear in the middle of a field.

A second popular explanation is that they are all hoaxed by two elderly gentlemen known affectionately as "Doug and Dave". There is also some merit in this explanation as undoubtedly some formations have been hoaxed. The next question has to be why are these things being hoaxed and what are these people copying? If there was nothing genuine to copy, there would be little sense in hoaxing them.

The government version is that these formations do not exist yet several farmers have been visited by black Ministry of Defence helicopters where the crew insists that a crop formation be ploughed over. More often than not these visits have occurred before the farmer knew that there was a formation in their field.

Whilst the vast majority of these formations appear in Britain, there are a growing number of reports from other countries. It could of course be that formations have always appeared world wide but were never noticed until recently, but this would be extremely unlikely.

Some formations have turned up in extremely unlikely places. There was one in the middle of a frozen lake in Sweden. This formation was made up of patterns cutting through the ice in the middle of the lake where the formation was surrounded by unfrozen water. Another formation in Sweden was where the top 60cm (2feet) of pine trees were bent into a very definite pattern in the middle of a very large plantation of 30m (100 foot) tall trees and could only be seen from the air.

There are other unusual features about genuine formations. The background radiation levels are usually measurably different in the middle of the formation. The crop itself has very often been laid down in extremely complex "stitching" patterns.

The crop is not flattened but bent, usually at "node" points. This is exceptionally difficult, if not impossible, to fake as the stalks tend to bend at their weakest point and not at the node which is the strongest. The node itself alters and very often has the appearance of being "burnt" and changed to a bright red in colour. The molecular structure of these nodes has also, usually, undergone a radical change.

The crop itself is usually not damaged but continues to grow and ripen in its normal way and can be harvested as normal. However, if the seed heads are collected and sown the following year, the crop yield is usually considerably higher than would normally be anticipated.

There are those who maintain that these formations must be formed by aliens and whilst it is an attractive, but romantic, theory, this is not the case. To begin to understand what these formations are and what they represent, we first have to look at where they are located.

Original research, being carried out by Steve Page and Glenn Broughton, shows that when the locations of these formations are plotted onto a map, several patterns begin to emerge.

By far the greatest concentration of formations appear, every year since 1990 except one, within a five mile radius of Avebury. In 1995 the epicentre shifted towards Winchester in Hampshire.

Virtually all of the formations, in Britain, have two identical characteristics. They all appear on or near a ley line and at least 80% appear on ground which has an underground aquifer. Aquifers are regions of underground rock, usually sandstone or similar, which hold and store water. Many of the country's towns are supplied with water drawn from these sources.

The other 20% would appear to be located on other water features. Water is well known to act as a "conduit" for energy. Ley lines, for example, will very often follow the course of underground streams.

What this research* all adds up to is that the crop formations all fall on energy lines or in regions where energy has accumulated in water or, quite often, both.

Human DNA is changing. We are undergoing our most radical shift of energies in our whole history. As our energies change

---

* For more information on this research, or for more information on crop formations in general, together with one of the world's largest data bases on crop formations, you can visit Steve Page and Glenn Broughton at their web site address which is: http://www.eclipse.co.uk/sacredcircle

so does our DNA. We are completing our final clearance of all the unwanted memories that we have stored away in our DNA over all of our many lifetimes. In order to complete this clearance we have to alter and increase our energy levels, the more energy we take on the more DNA we can clear, the more DNA we clear the more energy we can take on etc..

As we are undergoing our clearances and changes, so is the planet. The planetary consciousness is also having a clear out as its energies undergo a change equally as radical as ours. The planet's way of clearing out its accumulated debris is by forming swirls and patterns in its natural energy emissions which manifest themselves as crop formations.

There is also a second function to these crop formations. Several of these formations have included messages from the planet to us. A number of symbols have appeared which have stirred an ancient memory in many of the people who saw them. Several of the fractal type formations have been of patterns which have been produced by mathematicians.

This is why all of these formations follow energy lines or accumulations of energy and are concentrated around, what has traditionally been, the most powerful energy location on the planet.

We have mentioned, several times, that the planet's energies are changing and we should now take a look at this in greater detail.

The planet has always had its own energies. These are given form in the swirling magnetic flux which ebbs and flows with the way in which planetary life has been lived. As we arrived on the planet, we brought with us new frequencies of energy and worked with the planet's nurturing flow to enhance some of its work and to create new potential.

With the sinking of Atlantis, energy enhancements were added which provided a new source of life supporting energy.

Whilst we have been undergoing our information gathering sequential lifetimes, the old ley grid provided us with all of our needs. Now that we are close to the point of completing "The Human Plan", our needs are changing and with these new requirements comes the need for fresh and more powerful energies.

The old grid has been bent and manipulated, by those who knew how, into shapes and patterns that do not fit our new form and therefore, regrettably, much of this energy has had to be abandoned.

Many individuals and several organisations have worked with the old energies for their own purposes which have, at several times during human history, held us back or led us into some blind alleys. The overall affect upon our progression has not been great, but it has been noticeable.

Not all of these undesirable alterations can be easily removed as those who created these changes also created knots and eddies which cannot be untied. Where these difficulties exist, a new grid has been constructed.

This construction work has been carried out over the past fifty years by many individuals on a planet wide scale, with many of the "workers" totally unaware, on a physical level, what it was they were doing nor were they, generally, aware of the many "spirit" and non human helpers who assisted them.

Where the old grid could not be easily by-passed, all of the undesirable alterations had to be undone. Another army of workers dealt with these problems, again largely not knowing what it was they were working towards. All that they knew, physically, was that they were drawn to particular places and that they had to carry out certain tasks or particular meditations.

Most of these workers just knew that they were drawn to these places and when their work was finished, they moved on to other sites or resumed their normal lives. It was necessary to maintain an "operational silence" as these were everyday, normal people. Individuals who, if they had full knowledge of the work they were doing or of its' importance, would probably have crumpled under the weight of the magnitude of the responsibility.

To these individuals all of us, every single one of us, owe a great debt of gratitude. None of us would have been in a position to make our own changes if this work had not been completed.

So, what are the differences between the old grid and the new?

The old grid first came into being at the request of the planet towards the end of the Atlantis period. This grid worked with the planet's consciousness to enhance its life supporting energies. It also supplied us with a limitless source of energy to fuel our changing levels of awareness and existence.

This grid is that which we call the ley line network which spans and encompasses the whole planet. The ley lines themselves vary in their levels of energy and vary in their routes, according to the underlying ground structures. In most regions they follow underground water courses, sometimes man made water courses, or in dry areas, they tend to follow seams of quartz bearing rock.

It has been very easy to alter the flow and direction of the energies in this old grid. Houses or features built to span a ley line, for example, have been able to disrupt and even stop the free flow of energy. The Chinese art of Feng Shui is a perfect example of how these ley lines could be read and worked with to enhance the way in which we live. If we work with the energies, we can live more harmonious lives. If we ignore the energy, our lives can be disrupted in quite subtle, but important, ways.

It has been comparatively easy to manipulate, or even disrupt, these energy lines. Many buildings have been built across ley lines which have totally blocked the flow of energy. The flow can usually be re-instated quite simply by placing copper conductor rods or crystals into the ground around the building. The flow will then follow the line of the rods or crystals and connect in with the remainder of the ley line. Much of the repair work mentioned above has been of this nature.

Some of the disruption has been of a much more serious nature and has taken considerable effort to re-create a "clean" energy flow. There have been a number of organisations who have realised the potential of the grid and have used its energies for their own purposes. This kind of usage has been for purposes such as setting up miniature gateways. Most of these have been set up in small groups and have been used for secret travel between, for example, several buildings within a town. Essentially a network of secret "tunnels" mainly used to evade debtors or members of the judiciary.

Then there have been organisations whose aspirations have risen above purely local ambitions. These are organisations such as The Free Masons, The Knights of St John and, most widely known, The Knights Templar. These organisations, in the past, have set up huge global networks of energy gateways. Most have fallen into disuse and have been largely forgotten, however their influence on the grid has remained intact and a great deal of work has been carried out to undo the drain of energy that these networks created.

Most of these networks have fallen into disuse as the sphere of activities of these organisations has moved away from energy manipulation and into commerce. Over the past few years many individuals, world wide, have woken up to the fact that the planet's energies exist and that they have been manipulated by these organisations. There has been a great temptation to re-activate these networks by these individuals and the groups that have formed around them. Most of these individuals and groups had a previous lifetime working within the original organisations and have half remembered memories of their work with these private networks. It also serves to feed these people's egos, if I can re-open these gateways, it must mean that I am a "powerful" individual, or words to that effect.

In the misguided belief that re-activating these networks will help the planet, they have been actively working to re-open many of these gateways. These activities have a huge potential for disruption to the old and new grids.

All of these gateways have what is usually called a "black sentinel". The role of these sentinels is to protect a particular gateway and also to collect towards it any available energy source. Much of the work carried out by people to cleanse the old grid has been to close and seal these old gateways and lock away the black sentinels. The new global energy centres could only be switched on once these gates had been sealed. It was, literally, not possible before then. By other groups re-opening the old gates, disruption has occurred to the new grid and energy centres.

The black sentinels are a form of constructed "consciousness" who have been programmed to actively seek out new sources of energy. These "beings" are conglomerates of very sticky black energy. This does not make them "evil" in the sense that they are aware of carrying out "evil" acts, but are purely machines programmed to carry out particular tasks which they are very efficient at. By re-opening the old gates, the black sentinels are re-activated and their programming begins to run. Their first act is to essentially "hijack" the new energy sources and draw it into their grid.

On the face of it this might not appear to be much of a problem as the new energies are effectively limitless. However, they are causing disruption to the free flow of energy and have, in some instances, totally disrupted the new energy centres.

The best, and most public, example of the potential harm is with the new energy centre in Peru. All of the new energy centres were put into place at the start of "The Human Plan", over twenty thousand years ago. The sites were identified and their basic "wiring" put into place. They have remained dormant, not connected, since then.

Several of the organisations mentioned above were aware of the potential of these sites and positioned their own gates and sentinels at these locations with the view of making use of the energy centres when they were activated. The planned usage of these gates was to rob the new grid of their energies and divert it into the "private" networks. This would supply these organisations with a new limitless energy to feed their own schemes and to actively disrupt and slow down the process of completing "The Human Plan".

Over the centuries, many of these gates were prematurely opened by these organisations, or other individuals, for their own purposes. These purposes were not in the interests of mankind as a whole but to satisfy their greed for energy and manipulation. By opening these gates, it allowed the release of many of the undesirable elements of these organisations' activities. This is why these areas needed to be cleansed and the gates sealed.

With the sealing of these gates, the new energy centres could be fully connected and the new grid activated. Several of the groups, who have rekindled their past life connections with the private gateways, have been actively re-opening the sealed gates. Some have acted in a genuine belief that, by unsealing the old gates, they are helping the planet whilst some are well aware of the negative affects that their activities create. Whatever the motivation, the effects are the same: the black sentinels are released and their programming re-activated.

In South America there is a periodic reversal of the prevailing weather patterns, what has come to be known as "The El Nino Effect". The reversal is part of a normal pattern of weather which occurs about every ten years. This reversal gives South America monsoon-type rains, instead of their normal dry summers and gives countries such as Australia and Indonesia a drought instead of their normal rain. Over the past few years these patterns have begun to alter due to shifts in global weather patterns. However, part of the function of the new global energy centres is to stabilise and overcome some of the effects of global warming.

The gate close to the Peruvian energy centre was opened in 1997, shortly after the new grid was activated and the black sentinels have been diverting much of the energy into the "private" grid. This has had the effect of weakening the flow of energy from the energy centre into the new grid and, more noticeably, tended to hold the El Nino weather patterns in place.

The El Nino effect has not been caused by the opening of the private gate but it has had the effect of maintaining the weather reversal and increasing its effects resulting in the severe loss of life, crops and wildlife habitats on both sides of the Pacific Ocean.

There is nothing wrong with "tinkering" with the planet's energies, both old and new. We all have free choice and if we choose to "play" in this way then we are free to do so. However, the effects of some of this tinkering, presumably to satisfy someone's inflated ego, can and does have severe consequences.

We have free choice, but with that freedom comes the responsibility for our actions. We need to very seriously consider the effects that we will have before we undertake a particular course of action. The errors made with the Peruvian energy centre are very real.

As of August 12th 1998, the whole of the Templar grid, and other similar networks, have been destroyed. Their gates are totally sealed and the black sentinels dissolved. We now have a "clean" energy source, without any kind of drain or disruption. The whole of the energy network and the work involved in bringing about its completion is now proceeding as originally planned allowing our final stages of development to occur.

This does not mean that all of the sites are "clean". Some of the gates have been locked, but not fully destroyed. If you wish to "experiment" with these gates, then you should be aware that some still contain their black sentinels or other energy "traps". Remember, these gateways are designed to draw energy into themselves, from whatever source, if you are that source, then much of the energy of your chakras can be "stripped" and the implications of that occurring are too horrendous to contemplate. Be careful!

The old grid served its purpose very well. It has allowed us and the planet to fulfil all of the requirements that our choices asked of it. Despite the levels and types of interference, mentioned above, we have managed to maintain our potential and our plans.

134

Since the setting up of the grid, twenty eight thousand years ago, we have required a source of energy which was compatible with our own energy levels. Now that we are completing our plans and moving into an expanded awareness, a new source of energy is required.

The old grid has been comprised of levels of energy which were compatible with our energies whilst we were developing. These bands of energy spanned a frequency range of 7.56Hz to 250,000Hz, the human consciousness range. These frequencies contained up to forty three dimensions but the energy source, at Silbury Hill, contained a further seven dimensions to allow for fluctuating requirements. These were the energy ranges which related specifically to human requirements.

The planet's requirements took this range to over 1,000,000Hz and added another twenty five dimensions. All of this energy was contained within and distributed by the original seven global energy centres and the ley line network. The old grid was designed to comfortably accommodate all of these energy ranges.

With our changing awareness we, and the planet, require a different energy range. There are thirteen new energy centres which replace or work alongside the old seven. The primary energy centre's frequency range, when it was first connected, was 7.56Hz to 53,000,000,000,000Hz. Due to changing requirements and greater need, the higher end of the frequency range has risen to 375,000,000,000,000Hz. its dimensional spread is now from three to seven hundred and thirty eight. These figures, whilst basically meaningless to most of us, shows the magnitude of change in our requirements and capabilities.

The new grid connects in fully with the old grid. New sections have had to be formed where people's tinkerings have caused too much damage. Essentially, the old grid was totally upgraded to accommodate the changes and totally new sections of the grid were added to take energy to regions which had not been served before and to connect in with the new global energy centres.

The new energy centres and grid now contain all of our energy requirements to carry us through all of our current changes and well into the next phases of our development. The Orion gate, and the space contained within its enclosing envelope, has been altered to provide us with a much greater scope of activities and freedom of action.

We no longer need to be contained, but will be able to fly out to the stars.

Chapter Nine

The Process of Change

We are changing.

There is now, no longer, any doubt. The energy shifts that have been occurring since August 1996 are beginning to have their full effects and are showing up everywhere. The world is in turmoil, our bodies are in turmoil and our lives seem to be falling apart. And we have only really just begun!

This, however, does not mean that we are set for a future of unrest and grief, the exact opposite. We are at least half way through our final clearances and, once clear, there is no more. All that we need to do then is to allow ourselves to sit back and enjoy the final acts of our transitions and reap the full benefits of twenty thousand years of extremely hard work. You should be so lucky!

The opening sentence of this chapter sums the situation up - we are changing. Changing being the most important word. Up until now all of our work has been to bring us to a point where this change was possible.

We have now begun our change and, like all times of major change, there will be some uncomfortable elements. These uncomfortable parts of the process are, for some people, proving to be very traumatic, whilst for others, the changes are more easily dealt with.

We touched on some of these particular problems in chapter five, in this chapter we can begin to look at these in greater detail.

Our main region of change is within our personal energies. The chakras are undergoing a process of integration which takes us to places that we have never been before. Although, at the start of "The Human Plan", we were, consciously, fully integrated, because of the planet's unique energy structures we quickly began the slide to our lowest energy levels. The other problem was that as we were new to the planet we were so overwhelmed by its natural beauty and abundance of life that we were not fully aware of our potential place within it.

So, we are currently making our way to totally untrodden ground.

The importance of the changes taking place to the chakras cannot be stressed too highly. They are moving us from a purely physical being into a being of the universe. When the changes to the chakras are complete, we will incorporate all of the energy potential and knowledge that is contained within the Higher Self and be able to use it within our normal daily lives. Instant access to a universe of answers.

With the changes to our energies comes a change in the way in which the chakras function and the relationship they have with our physical organs. We looked at the new chakra colours in chapter five. This change of frequency also subtly changes their functions and their level of importance within our lives.

Each chakra relates very directly to an element of our consciousness, personality and our relationships with others.

The change of energy forces us to undertake courses of action which are, sometimes, quite alien to our usual nature. This is because we have tended to keep our true natures hidden and place around us false facades which are based upon the expectations of others. In other words, those with whom we share our lives anticipate that we will act in certain ways and, in order not to be ridiculed or rejected, we accept their expectations and fashion our lives and responses accordingly. This re-fashioning of ourselves has led to areas of severe conflict within our consciousness resulting in numerous and various illnesses.

As we take on board the new chakra energies this reinforces our original consciousness purpose and our false facades begin to be chipped away from the inside. No matter how much we try to resist the chipping away, we cannot. The truth of our being will always ultimately prevail. This is why so many people are undergoing a major re- structuring of their personalities at the moment and why so many questions are being asked. A new truth is emerging which is proving to be irresistible.

Major conflicts are arising which are tearing apart life long friendships and marriages. We are each undergoing this level of change at different rates. Each one of us is an individual and we are undergoing our transformations at a pace that is right for us. Nobody can dictate this rate of change for us. We have to move at our pace within our time.

Where one element of a friendship or a relationship begins to change then the other person involved has to adjust them-selves to the new situation or be left behind. If the person who is changing tries to hold themselves back major problems occur and whilst there is a certain degree of latitude in these changes, there comes a point where they cannot hold back any longer.

This is why so many friendships, relationships and marriages are falling apart. One of those involved begins to realise that they are changing. Their Higher Selves have realised that they are ready to accommodate the change of energy.

The best way to illustrate the problem is to go through the sequences involved.

It begins with a stirring, a feeling that deep inside, something is changing, you are not sure what, but something. You start to notice things about the people around you. Little things. Things which you have always accepted or not even noticed before begin to take on a significance, not too strongly to start with but, gradually, they begin to grate.

You begin to notice that the things people say to you are not strictly honest, you shrug them off to start with but you start to take more notice of them and find them less and less acceptable.

You start to notice advertisements for workshops on subjects which you have never noticed before, and then book yourself on one, as much to your surprise as anyone else's (or at least those you have trusted to tell). You begin to search out like minded people, those who are beginning to think in the same way as you.

Perhaps you seek out a healer or clairvoyant, possibly for the very first time, hoping for some understanding and guidance. You go to your first workshop and realise that there are others out there who are having similar new experiences and feelings. Some of these people you "connect" with on very deep levels. You start to graze through esoteric book shops, again perhaps for the first time. Titles leap out at you and you avidly devour the contents of these books but asking more and more questions as each of your earlier questions become answered.

Your friends and family start to look at you oddly, sometimes not meeting your eye or even beginning not to talk to you. Some might even suggest that you are becoming a little strange. You listen to this and begin to question yourself and what it is you are doing. You might be a bank clerk, a housewife, engineer, whatever, what on earth am I doing delving into "spiritual" matters? Am I strange? Am I wrong? Am I going completely loopy? But somehow you persevere and continue with your quest. Something inside has opened and will not shut or go away, no matter how much you might try.

You seek out other workshops or courses which allow you to explore yourself and your feelings in safe surroundings with other like minded people and, suddenly, emotions, which might have been very deep seated, come to the surface and you have to look at them and deal with them, perhaps for the very first time in your life. In these emotions you begin to realise your role within your life and the role that others have taken. These emotions begin to clear and you begin to feel lighter and freer.

You begin to delve deeper and deeper into yourself and your emotions and motivations, clearing as you go. It is not an easy process, sometimes extremely difficult and traumatic, but you continue. Your inner voice says YES, I AM RIGHT in what I am doing.

Your family and friends begin to express concern about you, some even become aggressive towards you.

You begin to question yourself again, are these people right, am I just being silly? But you know that you are right, somewhere deep inside, you know.

The more you clear yourself the more you realise that other people's reactions are not aimed at you, but at themselves. As you start to shine you begin to act as a mirror, reflecting people back at themselves. They no longer see you but themselves and they do not like what they see. They know that they should be undergoing the same changes as you but do not have the courage and this frightens them, makes them feel threatened. This person, you, who they have known for a long time has suddenly found the courage to change and they haven't. Are they missing out on something? Are they going to be left behind?

Eventually, those who have attacked you start to ask you questions, to borrow your books, maybe even go to their own workshops and they begin to change.

Their changing gives you more confidence and a fresh impetus and you seek out others, go to further workshops, read new books etc. and you move onwards. This then frightens your friends once more and the guilt/confidence cycle begins all over again. But this time, you have moved a little further forwards and it is not quite so threatening. You are more "centred" within yourself and criticisms and anger start to bounce off you. You feel lighter and freer than you have ever done in your life and you want more, almost to the point of obsession. As the new you emerges, you like what you see and cannot even begin to imagine how you put up with your old life or even how you could have lived at all in your old patterns.

The people around you take on less and less significance, not because you are becoming more selfish, but because they no longer make any kind of sense to you. You begin to make new circles of friends, those who think more like you and one day you wake up and realise that the old you no longer exists. All of your past has had to have been left behind, all of that emotional baggage has gone and with it some of the people you held dear. This is where the guilt and the pain begins again. Some of those you left behind you don't even think about, but some cause pain. You go back and try to talk to these people but you do not know where to start, or if you do they do not know how to answer the new you, they still seem to be stuck in their old patterns and refuse to budge. Perhaps you offer to help them to change but this offer is probably refused. So you move on.

By clearing out your debris and allowing your inner, dazzling light to shine, others begin to notice and think if you can do it, so can I, and a new set of cycles begin.

Gradually, more and more people begin their journeying. It is because of your courage that these people have begun to find theirs and make their first steps into themselves.
This is not people being selfish but finding the courage to face themselves and make the changes they know they have to make.

It is not easy, nobody can say that, but those who stand on the other side of themselves know who they are and that their journey was the ONLY path that they could have taken. So, wherever you are on your individual path, have courage, it will all soon become clear.

There are a second group of people who are also undergoing their energy changes, but in more subtle ways.

The ones described above are those who, in general terms, have had a certain amount of emotional debris, karma, to clear. These are people who made decisions in previous lifetimes where some elements of their personal plans were brought forward to this lifetime. For these people, the change is one of trauma as these old wounds are dealt with.

The second group of people are those who have brought very little or no karmic hangover.

For these, their transitions are a little different. Generally, they have led comparatively quiet lives with little or no major traumas. Their sexual relationships have been relatively calm and pleasant, their dealings with other people have been straight forward and uncomplicated and life, in general, has not been too difficult. This does not necessarily mean that they have sailed through life without any difficulties, but, where difficulties have arisen, they have been able to deal with them without too much drama.

These are people who have completed their individual parts of "The Human Plan" and are now in a condition where they are patiently waiting for the rest of the population to complete their own "plans".

This situation can also generate its' own traumas if it is not properly understood.

For these people, the questions they ask are along the lines of: if everyone is out there clearing their karmic debris and going through major trauma, why aren't I? This can cause some severe stress in some people. The fear is that they know that things are changing but because their lives are fairly straight forward and comparatively calm, they must somehow, somewhere be failing.

The way to determine if you are doing the right thing is to look back upon your lives in as honest a way as possible without letting the ego get in the way. How has your life been? Have you had major emotional battles? How difficult was it to achieve the goals that you had set yourself? How did other people respond to you? Was there aggression or just a quiet acceptance? How many people turned to you requesting that you be an "agony aunt"? It is how you respond to these questions that will help you to understand your current situation. It is no good giving answers that you hope are correct. You must be totally honest with yourself. Telling yourself lies will do you no good whatsoever, it never has, because now there is nowhere to hide from the truth.

If you can honestly answer these types of questions and answer yes to all of them, then the chances are that you have cleared everything that needs to be cleared. Nothing is happening in your life because nothing needs to happen, you have already done it.

If you have any no answers then it means that there are areas of your life which still need to be looked at. You cannot lie to yourself, nor can you ignore these areas of your life. In order to achieve your full transition, you need to be totally clear of all elements of your individual plan. Remember, you chose your particular path and it is no good complaining that you have more things to clear as it was you, and only you, that brought this situation about.

So look at yourself honestly. You are the only one who can judge and if it feels as though there is nothing to do, celebrate. Do not worry, you are of those few who have come to this life without a need to clear out any emotional baggage.

Just be patient a little longer.

There are other changes that take place within the chakras. Up until now they have all been of the same size, reflecting the equal importance of each element of our physical/consciousness connections. As the energy changes, so do the size of the chakras.

The karmic element of our lives has meant that so much of our time has been taken up by emotional problems. The vast majority of the body's organs have been directly influenced by the third chakra, personal power and emotional responses.

The liver, stomach, intestines, gall bladder, pancreas, spleen have all been under constant stress because of this relationship. This is the area of our lives which has been most affected by our highly charged lives.

As we clear ourselves of all of our emotional hurts and regain our own power, the role of this chakra begins to change and the chakra begins to reduce in size. It is purely and simply to do with the fact that this region of our lives takes on a lesser significance and our soul does not need to put such a high level of energy into this chakra. If we are emotionally clear and walking our "truth" then we do not collect any of the old emotional baggage.

The same is true for the second chakra. A high percentage of our emotional problems stem from our sexual relationships. When these issues also become resolved there is no need to divert so much energy into this chakra.

This is also why these areas of our lives are the ones which suffer the most as we begin our journey. There is more debris and rubbish connected with these two elements of our lives than with any other, they have to be cleared first and then the rest can follow.

The chakras take on the following relationships:

The root remains the same size, reflecting our continued commitment and connection to the planet.

The second and third chakras reduce by about one half in proportion to the root.

The fourth remains the same size reflecting our continued requirements to love ourselves and others. It will also continue with its primary function of connecting the higher energies into the physical energies.

The fifth chakra will also reduce in size as it becomes easier to express ourselves honestly and fully. its secondary role of communication will also reduce as the psychic communication centres in the brain become increasingly active (see below for more about this).

The sixth chakra remains the same size to reflect its growing importance in our changing spirituality and the increase in our psychic vision.

The crown also remains the same. The Higher Self might have been fully integrated, so the connection purpose is no longer required, but the amount of energy that the crown will accommodate will, possibly, make it grow in size.

There is another element to the change of energies which most of us will find a little uncomfortable to deal with, all be it temporarily.

Up until now we could, sort of, ignore our problems with not fully dealing with these consciousness issues. We could put them to one side and deal with them slowly, without too much harm coming to us, well, in the short term in any way. However, with the huge acceleration in our energies, we will no longer have the luxury of time. As we rapidly change our energy structures, any hurt to our chakras, either by ourselves or others, will be immediately felt and the hurt itself will demand to be dealt with.

Fortunately, this situation will not last for too long. As more and more people undergo their own clearances, the opportunity for this kind of harm will rapidly diminish and eventually disappear.

On other, more physical levels, other changes are taking place as a consequence of the change of energies.

We have already mentioned the changes to the DNA in chapter five. These changes have been noted by the medical profession, over the past ten years, with a growing amount of concern. The problem is that discoveries made in any of the sciences, once they have become accepted by the establishment, usually after a great deal of fighting and back biting, end up being carved in stone, or at least until the ideas that were considered crazy a few years ago are accepted as obvious.

Once they have reached the stone mason, any variation or deviation from this accepted norm is seen as something negative. Medicine ignores the most important element of any individual, that is their consciousness. Science does not have a way of explaining what makes you, you or me, me. They only see the mechanics of the body and not the extreme beauty of its inner workings. If all you see is a mechanical collection of disassociated body parts, then any change to the accepted model is a concern.

Medicine cannot explain the meaning of 90% of DNA, but their arrogance has led them to name it junk, neither can they explain about the same proportion of the workings of the brain, and yet this does not stop them claiming that they know everything there is to know about the body.

The truth is it is consciousness that determines the function of every organ and our genetic structures act purely on the directives of our consciousness.

Body part location is only a small part of the role of our DNA. It is our primary memory system and everything that we have ever been or we have ever experienced is stored away in there. As we undergo our change, we are able to deal with a greater proportion of our total memory and, therefore, our memories are returning, that is, our DNA is re-combining.

There are, inevitably, pitfalls in this particular process. Stored away in the DNA is a memory of every illness that we have ever suffered. As the DNA begins to re-combine, every memory that is no longer required has to be removed. Again, this is not a question of may be, but must be. As the virus etc. leaves the DNA it makes its way out through the body's cell structures and organs. If there is any uncleared debris in the associated organ, the virus can have an infecting affect on that organ. This is why we have seen the rise of so many "unknown" viruses in the recent past. They are not unknown, just forgotten.

Some of these viruses respond to modern antibiotics, some do not. Regardless of medical treatment, these viruses will not fully leave the body until the associated chakra trauma is dealt with. This does not usually present any major problems (see below for more detail about this aspect of clearance) as the infected individual has to be a long way down their clearance path for this depth of memory to have been dislodged.

This is also the main reason why medical treatments are increasingly ineffective. If it was possible to remove these memories from the body by taking a pill, there would be no value in the clearance as it would tend to remove personal responsibility. As the problem arose by ignoring this responsibility in the past, the problem would not be cleared and would manifest itself somewhere else in the body.

Whilst on the topic of chakras and clearances, there is another way of looking at your personal situation.

The more energy that we absorb, the more the body has to clear itself. Sometimes this kind of clearance manifests itself as physical illness. As was mentioned above, we used to be able to absorb our hurts into the body's tissues where they could lie dormant for many years. As is true for the world around us, the world inside of us has many dark corners. As we take on more and more energy, these dark corners become illuminated and these hurts and potential illnesses must be released.

Many of us are coming down with unusual illnesses. We look at all forms of treatment which would seem to offer help. Some do help to relieve the symptoms whilst others do not make any difference. We start to look at our lives and begin to question what it is we are doing. If I am "walking in my path" why am I ill? I have improved my nutrition, turned away from harsh medical treatments (prescribed drugs), I have taken up drumming, dancing, acupuncture, healing, whatever, and yet I am still ill. I was perfectly healthy before I started!

The only way of fully understanding this situation is to approach the problem through the consciousness, the soul. All of who we are, or should be, is represented by the chakras. The chakras are the only totally accurate diagnostic tool that we have. Every one of our hurts are stored away within specific bodily organs which relate directly to a particular chakra. As we take on board our new energies, we also begin to cleanse the chakras. Any and all uncleared or undealt with issues have to be released. You were not actually healthy before you began to take on your new energy, it was just easier to hide the symptoms. Now that your energies are changing, these symptoms can no longer be hidden.

Look at the list of the chakras and related organs in chapter five and relate your symptoms to the corresponding chakra. Then look at which areas of the consciousness this chakra relates to. Each has a primary and secondary function. One or other of these functions have not been expressed fully in the past and the hurt to the chakra is letting itself be known by manifesting physical symptoms which relate to the corresponding bodily organs or systems.

The best way of explaining how this works is to look at how some real symptoms relate to chakra trauma.

Irritable Bowel Syndrome

This is a "blanket" medical term which is used to describe a variety of ailments which the doctors cannot trace to any particular source. The symptoms are usually pain in the abdominal region which ranges from a mild discomfort to severe spasms of pain.

If you look at the chakra list you will see that this region of the body relates to the third, or solar plexus, chakra. This chakra's primary function deals with issues involving personal power, issues such as whether your boss at work or your partner at home takes you seriously. The secondary function is the emotions.

The organs covered by this chakra are the liver, gall bladder, stomach, pancreas, spleen and the intestines. The liver is the master organ in this region of the body and stores away all of the reactions and emotions covered by the chakra that we did not express. The liver then distributes these unexpressed emotions to appropriate organs. The gall bladder deals with anger. If we do not express our feelings of anger then it becomes lodged here affecting the amount of bile which is discharged into the intestines. Too little bile and we create constipation.

The stomach deals with issues which we literally could not stomach, situations which were too much for us to accept.

The pancreas deals with the force with which we responded to these issues. If we responded too gently then the residue of the wanted response becomes lodged here affecting our blood sugar levels.

The spleen deals with the frustration connected with our unexpressed anger. This affects blood cleansing and parts of the endocrine system and also the stomach as vitamin B12 levels drop.

The intestines deal with issues we have not cleared from our past. We are literally hanging onto the "debris" of the past (there is a four letter word which describes this better, but it would be inappropriate to use it in these pages).

So, problems with this region of the body relate very specifically with our not expressing our hurts, angers and emotions. There are several ways of dealing with these problems. You can turn your whole attitude around and start to regain your own power, but it would be fair to say that this is the most difficult route. You can use a chakra balancing meditation which allows you to explore these specific organs. By exploring within in this way it is possible to look at these issues, bundle them up in an energy ball and throw them out through the chakra. This does clear this kind of debris very well. The third approach is to become angry in a place which you feel comfortable in. Just scream and shout as much as you can to let this stuff out. The gentlest approach is to make a giveaway. This is an American Indian tradition where you write down all of your hurts and angers onto paper and burn the paper. You can also write them down on the beach and let the tide wash them away.

In doing all of these exercises you are releasing and letting go of the emotion. As you clear the chakra, its energy stabilises and becomes clearer and stronger. As the chakra strengthens, it will allow less and less debris in, making you stronger and begin to regain your own power.

Breast Cancer

This is a very emotive subject which engenders fear in many people. Although it is usually women who have this problem, it is not unknown in men. More usually, men have heart attacks or angina as their version of this type of chakra trauma.

This region of the body is covered by the heart chakra which deals with how we express our love. This is how we express love for ourselves or for others. The organs affected are the heart and circulatory system, the immune system and the endocrine system.

Breast cancer comes from problems with the endocrine system. This system deals with cleansing toxins out of our physical tissues particularly through the lymphatic glands and the thymus. The lymphatic system is nearly as extensive as the blood system. Problems occur as we have been unable to express love for ourselves and this is why it relates more to women than to men. Our society expects women to put themselves down in favour of taking on someone else's problems. Women are always someone's daughter, someone's girlfriend, someone's wife and someone's mother, they are never allowed to be themselves. If women do begin to fight for themselves, they are considered selfish.

This wound to women becomes stored within the lymph glands across the chest and under the arms. If this toxic debris is not allowed to be cleared, it builds up pressure within the glands and results in abnormal cell growths.

The best way of clearing this problem is to find some time for yourself. This can be as little as an hour a week as long as it is remembered that this time is for you. You do not use this time to do something for anyone else. You have to be strong in this. It is the intent with which you approach all of these problems which make the difference more than any other factor. A change of attitude is required on a fundamental level. You are finding time for you, that is all that matters. It does not matter about the children, the cooking, the ironing, the washing up, etc. You are the most important person of all and you have to let your family know that you are making this change to your life. If you can be strong in this then they will accept this change. Be selfish for the first time in your life, buy yourself some flowers, give yourself a treat. Not for anyone else, but for yourself. Acknowledge to yourself that these little treats are for you, this time is for you and your whole world and health can change. Once you have begun this course, you cannot waver from your resolve. Do not let anything detract from your time, read a book during the day, watch your favourite soap, whatever, it is your time and nothing or anybody is allowed to encroach upon it. Be strong.

The male version of this type of problem is that they do not express their love for others very easily. Again, it is social conditioning which is largely responsible for this attitude. These attitudes manifest themselves by a hardening of the muscles of the heart. In a mild form this can result in angina or a stroke. Where these warning signs are ignored, they can result in a heart attack. Again, the only solution is to alter the intent with which you approach these problems. You need to let go and express your feelings for others in much more open and deeper ways. Meditations, of the type mentioned above, can help but it is the change in attitude which is the most important.

The second chakra

This is the part of our consciousness which primarily deals with our creativity and secondly with our sexual relationships. The two aspects very often go together. Those who are very artistic are often very sexually active whilst those in suppressive relationships are not usually very creative.

154

Where suppression exists, this usually results in ovarian/uterus problems in women, usually leading to hysterectomy and prostate/testicular cancers in men. Both male and female conditions which have dramatically increased in recent years. Women's problems usually arise from troublesome relationships whilst men's problems usually stem from lack of creativity.

This should be a clue as to how to deal with these problems. With women, this does not necessarily mean that you must walk away from your partner, although this can sometimes be the only answer, but you can deal with these issues by taking up a creative hobby. It does not make the whole problem go away but it does begin to deal with some of the primary issues. The same solution also applies to men, be more creative.

Persistent coughs

Many people are finding that they have "colds" and catarrh which hang on for months at a time and cannot be cleared fully. There has also been a return of tuberculosis (TB) recently. These conditions relate to the fifth, or throat, chakra. This chakra deals with self expression and communication. If we do not express ourselves properly and fully, we create a blockage in the chakra resulting in a blockage in the lungs, throat or even the thyroid gland. A way of clearing these kinds of conditions is to begin to "speak your truth", express yourself more fully. Tell people what you think instead of swallowing your tongue. Sometimes, singing classes can be extremely helpful in clearing these blockages as can Alexander Technique exercises which are designed to "open up" the chest.

It would be fair to say that most of the situations discussed here relate to women. There is a very good reason for this, women have been totally suppressed for many centuries by a male dominated society. By women accepting the situation, they have buried away their hurts and angers which has resulted in the need to clear out so many problems in this lifetime.

This is not intended to be a sexist comment, but a realistic look at the last few hundred years of human history. Every single person, born since the end of the First World War, has been taking part in an exercise designed to rid women of these buried problems. Men, generally, have acted in the way that they have in order to force women to react. Throughout the whole of "The Human Plan" we have chosen to place ourselves into situations which have required us to struggle and fight. It has been in this way that we have learned our limitations and how to overcome them. By men taking on the role of the aggressor it has forced women to fight back. This has finally led to the position we find ourselves in today, women are rapidly regaining their own power and making their own choices. This is something which was not possible one hundred years ago.

As we undergo this final act of balancing, men are also beginning to change. However, their change is proving to be one which, in many ways, is much simpler. Essentially, what men are learning to do is to let go. They have held control for a very long time and have been reluctant to relinquish their position but, at long last, they are starting the process.

This letting go produces its own set of health problems but these are mainly psychological instead of physical. There has been an increase in domestic violence recently which reflects the male problem. If you are used to holding power then anyone trying to take it from you is a threat and many men are responding to this threat by acts of violence. Not all men are behaving in this way. Many men have arrived in this lifetime prepared for this re-balancing and are actively working towards this goal.

Remember, we have chosen our roles in all of our lifetimes and this includes the choice of being either male or female. Everything that has happened to us has happened because we chose it to happen. The turmoils being experienced in this lifetime are of our choosing. If we all understood this basic fact of life, then we could make all of our transitions much more easily. By taking responsibility for our actions, in the past, the present becomes much easier.

The other group of individuals which are experiencing major difficulties are children. Many of these individuals have been born with the new energies intact and with no, or very little, karmic debris.

In the past, childhood illnesses, those that were contracted before puberty, were almost entirely due to problems carried forwards from previous lifetimes. Whilst there is still a certain amount of this, for example the major cause of childhood cancers is past life clearances, the vast majority of current childhood illnesses are caused by current lifestyles.

Do not forget that children are not new souls but old souls inhabiting a new body. This fact is very easy to forget as we only see the unformed human and not the ancient conscious-ness that formed the body. Their inexperience relates only to this current lifetime. Recently, many children have been born with their experience and wisdom intact at birth and are, if anything, more "advanced" than their parents.

The most prevalent childhood illness is currently asthma. Although the chakras are not fully formed until puberty, they are still a good indicator of where these illnesses come from. With asthma, the child is not being allowed to express themselves fully.

The reasons for this are usually quite complex but most can be tracked down to the way in which we expect our children to live. In the past, we allowed children free range of their outside environment. This allowed them to interact fully with other children and find out who they were as individuals by finding their own ways of self expression. The general perception, at the moment, is that abduction, violence and paedophilia is on the increase and, therefore, children are increasingly being denied their freedoms. If you take a look at crime records, or at least for as far as these records go back, you will see that crimes of this nature have remained at a fairly constant level. In other words, children today are no more at risk of these crimes than their parents were or their grandparents were. The main cause of our incorrect perceptions appears to be the media. They apparently feel that there is something to be gained from spreading this kind of story over the front pages, whereas all it really does is paint a very distorted view of the world.

Whilst there are other aggravating factors, such as car pollution, the real underlying cause of illnesses such as childhood asthma is the denial of the child's expression of themselves. As these children reach puberty they have a distorted view of the world brought about by being cocooned in this way. This can create many unnecessary problems and lead to severe insecurities as they are cleared.

The best way of dealing with these problems is to help children find ways in which they more fully interact with other children and not put them in front of the TV or a computer screen. Remember, we have chosen all of the major experiences which we encounter in life. If we have chosen to be abducted, sexually assaulted, etc. then it will occur regardless of the restrictions we place on our or other's movements. As we complete our transitions into the new energies, the less and less we need learning experiences of this type and the crime rate will continue with its current decline.

The solutions discussed above might sound a little simplistic but remember, we are dealing with the fundamental issues underlying health problems.

Any treatment taken for these conditions can, theoretically, deal with the symptoms. The symptoms will disappear for a while but will then return, often more virulently than their first manifestation. How many people have you come across who have had a serious condition, such as cancer or a heart attack, which has responded to the treatments given, only to find that they have a return of the condition which then kills them? This is due to the underlying issues and associated chakra trauma not being dealt with. How many people have you come across who have, as a result of serious illness of the type given above, changed their attitude to their lives and never had the illness again? These are the people who have dealt with the underlying issues.

It is not being suggested that these conditions should not be treated, the symptoms do need to be cleared by whatever method the individual chooses, but if the underlying causes are not dealt with then the condition will return. The speed of return will vary from individual to individual but return they will and as our energies accelerate the speed of the return is also accelerating.

This could be seen as the negative side of our personal changes. Once we made the decision to complete our chosen part in "The Human Plan" we began to take on board the new energies. As these energies began to enter our chakras, we began to cleanse ourselves. If you have any illnesses then it is because you have areas of your life which need to be dealt with and resolved. Before we made our decisions, there was an opportunity to ignore these issues and chakra traumas, now that we have begun to accelerate, we can ignore them no longer.

When these issues are dealt with, we rapidly change to more positive pursuits.

As we clear ourselves to deeper and deeper levels, it allows us to take on higher and higher levels of energy, which allows us to clear deeper and deeper levels, which allows us to take on higher and higher levels of energy etc.. As we take on more and more energy, more and more of our DNA re-combines allowing greater and greater access to our memories and that which is the essence of us. When we arrive at the point where we have successfully re-combined seven strands of the DNA we will again accelerate. This is the final acceleration and will allow us to take on board all of our consciousness and to re-combine all of our DNA making us very different beings to those we are now.

We are unable to fully comprehend the magnitude of this change as we are unable to, as yet, access the memories of our time before the beginning of "The Human Plan".

Life will never be the same again.

There are other, more physical changes that we are also beginning to notice. The two most important, and the most noticeable, are connected with changes within the brain.

We have always retained the capacity for psychic, thought wave, communication. We have, largely, forgotten about this capability up until now. The psychic communication centres are located in the parietal lobe of the brain. This is a region towards the top of the head and just behind the line of the ears. Another, associated region is the occipital lobe which is located at the very back and lower region of the brain. These regions are in both hemispheres.

As these regions begin to wake up, they have begun to expand and the skull has also had to expand to accommodate this change. This expansion has caused, literally, a great many headaches in the recent past and will continue to cause headaches for the near future. This does not mean that these headaches will become a permanent feature, but their frequency will gradually wear off as we begin to settle into our new condition of being.

A second problem associated with this expansion process is that the muscles at the back of the neck will tend to become stretched. The muscles most affected are the levator scapulae, the rhomboid minor, the trapezius and the nuchal ligament also the suprahyoid muscles and the sternocleidomastoid muscle in the front and side of the neck. This also results in headaches, as well as a stiff neck and shoulders. The best way of dealing with these headaches is to take, at each individual's discretion or state of health, small dosages of paracetamol, preferably nothing stronger. A good gentle massage is also helpful and very relaxing.

The second region where problems are being experienced is in the jaw. There are two reasons for this, the first is that there is a meridian which runs from the top of the head and down the neck, its route passes through the nerve centre at the junction of the jaw with the skull.

This meridian is now having to accommodate higher levels of energy flow that it has in the past and it is "aching" slightly as it adjusts.

The main reason for jaw pain, however, is that there is a main neural pathway that runs through the jaw nerve centre. This collection of nerves is also having to deal with a much higher level of activity than it has in the past.

This activity mainly comes from a general increase in all of the brain's activities as it tries to work with the DNA and energy changes. The crown chakra works directly with the upper brain and the sixth chakra works directly with the lower brain. As the energies of these chakras changes, so does the activity in these regions of the brain. The changes in our DNA also mean that the brain itself is changing in structure and taking on board several new functions to accommodate our heightened levels of awareness.

The result of these changes is periodic pain in the jaw and in the teeth. There is very little that can be done to alleviate these pressures as these physical changes have to occur at their own pace to suit the changing capabilities of the individual concerned.

Again, low dosages of pain killers is the quickest method of dealing with these symptoms.

Do not worry, these discomforts will not last for very long and will gradually disappear.

There are further ways in which these problems can be eased. A dietary supplement of potassium can help. Potassium is a mineral which the body uses to build nerve tissue. By increasing the body's potassium levels with a daily intake of additional potassium, the nerve stresses can be helped and the headaches minimised. Another, secondary cause of these conditions, especially the headaches, is a reduction in blood sugar levels. As we take on the new energies, the body's metabolism also rises. This increases the amount of glucose that we need to live our ordinary lives. Daily intakes of high glucose drinks, especially the isotonic types, can help to rapidly replace blood glucose levels. Intakes of chocolate, fruit and alcohol can, unfortunately make the situation worse, despite their high natural sugar content. The high glucose, isotonic type drinks are rapidly absorbed into the blood stream and can help considerably in our physical energy levels and reduction in head, neck and jaw pains.

The most important thing of all to remember is that we are undergoing a natural process, a process which we began twenty thousand years ago. The pains which we might have to deal with are transient and will last, at most, a few months and usually a lot less than that.

Think of them as growing pains, as we adjust to the greater, renewed us. To be in a position to suffer these pains means that we are alive and well down our chosen path. Nothing is happening to us that we did not ask to happen and nothing is happening that we are not equipped to deal with.

Do not lose heart just because your head aches for a while, we have taken twenty thousand years to arrive at this point and our journeys are almost complete.

Chapter Ten

The Symptoms of Change

It is all very well talking about changes and their effects on our world and our lives when for a number of people these are not issues which they have begun to think about.

What changes? Where am I in all this? Where do I fit into the scheme of things?

We need to take a look at the world around us and the affects that are beginning to show.

To begin with, we can look at politics.

In Britain, the political position has recently undergone a radical change in philosophy. We have changed from a right wing government of seventeen years to a new left wing government who were elected for promising a radical approach.

This might not sound like a major change but if you look at the underlying reasoning then we have undergone one of the largest changes in the past fifty years.

The first and second world wars totally altered the world and the way in which people interacted with each other and how the world was viewed. Since then we have, basically, followed a confrontational approach in our political parties. There has been radical change but usually away from the beliefs of one party in order to, temporarily, accept the beliefs of another.

Lately, we have had one party totally dominate political thinking. Their term in office has gone against the post war pattern of voting. This reflected a need for stability and, more importantly, a need to investigate the more materialistic approach to life. In some respects, this was the final throes of the old world. Grab what you could whilst the opportunity was there and not worry about the consequences.

Essentially, an extremely selfish, unthinking and uncaring society. A demonstration of what was the worst in the human character. We needed a lesson in excess in order to realise that it was possible to create a balance. By demonstrating that the selfish pursuit of money was destructive to the planet and all of its peoples, it brought us to our senses and made us realise that we have other responsibilities.

The change of government reflects that change of attitude. This does not mean that the new government is any better, its first year in office showed that it was not fundamentally different to the previous one. Their election reflected our growing need to distance ourselves from a purely materialistic approach.

Around the world very many countries have undergone a similar, and usually more violent, change.

The whole change began with the overthrowing of the apartheid regime of South Africa. Think of the courage and sacrifice it took to achieve that. This was closely followed by the tearing down of the Berlin wall and the change of attitude and opening up of ideas that that entailed. The Soviet countries were torn apart, resulting in civil war and the clearance and settling of old scores and debts. Yugoslavia underwent the same process and showed up the brutality that underlies those who wish to hold onto power. Northern Ireland finally found a way to bring peace, albeit an uneasy truce.

China has been rocked by civil revolt and a very clear message that reform must take place or even that regime must fall. Indonesia's young could not accept their country's leaders, or their deceit and excesses, any longer and brought down a government that most thought could never be toppled. The list goes on as most countries undergo their own versions of the same events.

People are taking control of their own lives and if their political leaders do not change, then the people will change them. The message is simple, no longer will we tolerate those who act against us. This is true on personal, political and national levels. People are re-discovering their voice and their power.

We have also seen an incredible increase in armed conflicts in very many countries.

The karmic accounts have to be balanced.

There are several ways of achieving this. Where governments have begun to become "enlightened", these old scores have been settled by negotiation. Sometimes a show of force has also been necessary to aid the negotiations, but these disputes have been settled relatively amicably.

However, in some regions, the karmic hurt has been held onto very tightly and those involved have not been prepared to let go. It has been in these regions that wars have broken out.

Israel, Yugoslavia, Ethiopia, The Sudan etc. are all regions where this kind of unenlightened approach has prevailed.

These conflicts cannot continue. There is, unfortunately, no magic wand that can be waved that will stop these people acting in their destructive ways. Eventually, as in Northern Ireland, the mass consciousness will change to a more positive approach and these conflicts will gradually peter out. It might seem impossible at the moment, but the changes of attitude that have already occurred are a good indicator that this level of change is possible.

There are also changes on very many other levels.

Vast numbers of people are turning away from the traditional religions. For many, they are finding that their own answers make more sense and do not feel the same need to worship. There is a greater acceptance of a Creator, but with that acceptance comes the understanding that we are a part of that ultimate source and, therefore, worship is unnecessary. For others, there is total rejection of any religious doctrine.

For some, they are turning to new religions that they feel reflect their changing view and changing needs in more appropriate ways.

Some are returning to the original precepts of their religion and turning away from the large amount of changes that have been added over the centuries to suit political moods. This fundamentalist approach also reflects the search for the underlying truth.

Then there are those who feel lost and confused because they feel that the belief system that they were brought up in does not answer their current questions. For these people they are beginning their search anew and are starting to find new answers for themselves.

Others are hanging onto their old beliefs, not because they necessarily still feel them to be correct, but in a changing world these beliefs are familiar. It is this familiarity which gives them a sense of continuity and stability whilst everything else in their lives is in a state of change.

Whatever our religious beliefs, we are starting to realise that they can no longer give us the answers that we need in our changing world.

Our view of our world is also undergoing a radical change.

Up until now, we have accepted the official view that everything exists in separate "worlds". If we hacked down millions of acres of rainforest on the other side of the world it would not affect us in any way, except to fill someone's pockets.

Finally, we are beginning to realise that everything is connected and inter-related. The total loss of one species in one part of the world can have far reaching repercussions for other species in other parts of the world.

The dumping of our waste at sea has caused tremendous harm before it washes up on someone else's shores and still has to be disposed of correctly.

We have finally realised that the oceans are our life blood and keep us alive. Poisoning them slowly poisons us.

We have allowed our food to become a source of illness and disease.

Adding antibiotics to animal food is gradually breaking down our immune systems and leaving us open to medically incurable diseases.

The use of chemical sprays and pesticides is slowly filling our bodies with poisons, both directly and indirectly. The harshness of the chemicals and the level of deposits within the body, both human and animal, is causing the breakdown of our cell structures and producing genetic abnormalities.

We are deliberately adding the genetic structure of one species into the genetic structures of another. Bearing in mind that, by their own admission, the scientific community does not know what 90% of our DNA is for, this has the potential to cause damage on an unprecedented scale and return us to the worst excesses of the end of Atlantis. At least in Atlantis we were aware enough to know the outcome of our experiments and, even then, they led to the destruction of the human race, as it then existed, and the removal of a continent.

We have started to say no. The growth in demand for organically produced food is gradually taking over from chemical farming and it is by choosing this form of food that we can stop these dangers from progressing any further. Many people are returning to the old ways of growing vegetables and turning their back gardens into vegetable plots where they have control over what chemicals, if any, are used.

Our approach to our health is also rapidly changing. There is a growing rejection of harsh chemical treatments which cause as much harm as good. The philosophy of prescribing one pill to counteract the side effects of another prescribed pill is rapidly being rejected.

Instead, we are turning to gentler forms of assistance and consulting the diverse range of "alternative" practitioners which are now available. This switch reflects our growing understanding of our bodies and the recognition that we have to take responsibility for our own health.

As we clear ourselves on deeper and deeper levels, the more we understand ourselves and we are less willing to hand our bodies over to those who see them as only a collection of dis-associated parts.

As we are making our change of understanding so is, very slowly, the medical institution. We are gradually seeing the availability of alternative treatments at hospitals and surgeries. A growing number of doctors are referring their patients to homeopaths, accupuncturists, aromatherapists, healers etc. and patients are getting better instead of getting worse.

It has again been people exercising their freedom to choose that has brought these changes about.

Scientific understanding is also undergoing change, albeit at a slower pace. Those who have put themselves forward as investigators of the truth seem to have had remarkably closed minds.

The investigation of psychic phenomenon has at last begun. Reluctantly, but at least it is a start.

New theories and new proofs are tearing down many of the wrongly held beliefs that have helped to hold us back. There is a closing of the chasm that kept religion and science apart. The leading edge of science, quantum physics, is gradually realising that our universe could not exist if, somewhere, a "mind" did not believe that it does. This understanding is taking its time to be accepted, after all, most scientists believe that we are no more than a random collection of electrical and chemical impulses. As they cannot explain consciousness they tend to deny its existence.

The more that we clear ourselves, the more that we can "feel" the truth of situations and what others say. This is why we

170

are listening to the scientific community less and less and making up our minds for ourselves.

In all aspects of our lives people are making themselves heard. We no longer blindly accept the views of others but decide our lives for ourselves. We are taking back control of us.

Many of us find this prospect a little frightening, after all we have become used to letting others make decisions on our behalf. But everywhere we look this situation is changing. It might only be in small ways, such as complaining about receiving poor service from shops etc., but it is a start and each time we take back our own power the stronger we become.

It is little steps like these which change worlds.

As you read this chapter, it sounds as though we still have a very long way to go. It might seem that way, but the truth is very different.

The main indicator of change is in our energy structures and the way in which our DNA responds to this change.

Over the past ten years, for some individuals it is even longer, children have been born with a number of their old/new abilities intact. Many midwives have reported that a large number of the children they have delivered have a look in their eyes which says that they know who they are and why they are being born. It is a look of old wisdom.

As these children have grown older, they have found that many memories of past lives, and the knowledge gained, is intact and readily accessible.

Many have been born with three, sometimes four, strands to the DNA helix intact, sending shock waves around the medical world. With this DNA often comes the new energies. These children do not just have the old chakra colours but sparkle and glow with the new.

Many adults have also reached this stage in their transitions. The author, in his healing work, has the ability to see energies and to scan the body to a level where DNA can be read. Many patients who have come for healing, over the past few years, have begun their DNA changes and some have taken on board up to 60% of the new energy.

There are a number of people, worldwide, who have five DNA strands and up to 80% of the new chakra colours.

Change is happening on a vast scale. We can no longer sit back and ignore it.

Every one of us has the ability to change and to complete our transitions. If you feel as though you have only just begun your transformation, don't worry, you are not going to be left behind. Neither does it mean that you will have to experience major clearances in a very short time. Just because things feel as though they are slow to change, it does not mean that they actually are. We are all changing at a pace that is appropriate to us, when the time is right, the Higher Self will do what it needs to do and complete the job. All we can do in the mean time is to work on issues as they arise and explore new possibilities as they present themselves.

We can do no more than that. Oh! and don't panic.

For those who ask: we are on track.

In the early hours of the 1st of November 1998, a new "wave" of energy was released from the thirteen global centres. This new energy has the intention, and the power, to sweep away the final residues of the old. With this energy comes a final cleansing of karmic energy. As this tidal wave makes its way around the globe, the whole global energy will change to a positive role. By the end of the year 2,000 the process will be complete and our world can never return to the darkness of the last 7,000 years.

Chapter Eleven

The Fool's Final Steps

There is an old American Indian expression which states that before you criticise another you should walk a mile in their moccasins.

What this expression means is that we each have lived our own lives, nobody else has determined our path. We have had, and continue to have, absolute free choice in everything that we do, individually and collectively. Before we comment on another's actions we should take the time to see the world and their life as they see it. Their choices have led them into certain directions. Our lives, and the choices we made to determine those lives, have led us in directions of our own. Nobody has a right to judge us nor do we have a right to judge them.

We have travelled many miles and taken many first steps to arrive at this point in time. Fool or otherwise, we have arrived at our final steps before we begin a new cycle of life. For some, those first steps begin again. For others, it is time to stand still and take stock. For the rest of us, it is our choice to walk onwards to take ever more first steps until we arrive at our destination. Nobody has determined our path other than ourselves.

What we have achieved, by all of us fools ending our walk at the same time and at the same place, is beyond measure. Nobody has ever stood where we are standing and it will be a very long time before anybody will again.

The achievement cannot be underestimated. We have taken on a task that many throughout the universe thought was impossible. The early mistakes of Atlantis, the stumbles along the way all added up to what appeared to be an impossible task. Humanity should not exist. All of the odds have been stacked against us.

To understand what it is we have done, we need to take several steps backwards and take a look at ourselves from the viewpoint of an outsider. Who are we really? Do any of us have the definitive answer? Or do we have only our answer? Could our observer really understand who we are and what it is we have achieved? I think not.

Our collective consciousness holds the keys to who we are and that which we are about to let go of.

The other question is of course, does it really matter? What is it that we actually add up to? Can I, as an individual, really have been a part of this process? Did I really take all of those steps over these many centuries? The answer to that is yes and YES again.

Collectively, whilst remaining an individual with total free choice, we have acted together in the ultimate experiment and won through.

Twenty thousand years of our existence is now at an end and this is what we find most unbelievable. We have fought, pleaded, surrendered and overcome all odds to arrive at this point, where we can begin to look on our journeys with a final understanding.

The planet and our own consciousnesses have not allowed us to take this view before. To have done so, until we were finally ready, would have undone all of our past work. Since those very early days when we first arrived on the planet, we are complete and we cannot ever be fragmented again.

For those who have chosen to stand still they need to take stock of who they are and why they stopped their journey. Those who have decided to start again, on another world, need to ask themselves where did their courage fail. Now, at the end of all our work, is the time when we most need to question.

So, where do we go from here, assuming that here is a place that has further paths to take. Only you can answer that question.

We all have our own pair of moccasins.

Author's Note

"The Fool's First Steps" is, in some respects, a sequel to *"The Journey Home"* and was written partly in response to questions raised by readers of the first book and at the workshops and talks that we have given.

The second book, jointly written with my wife Diane, is *"The Healing Book"* and is the healing course that we teach in a written form. The book also contains a description and method of approach of some the more advanced healing techniques we use in our "psychic surgery" healing practice.

In reading these books, many people have found the answers to most of their current questions. However, they have also brought up some new ones.

The research carried out to produce these books, a sort of surfing through the human mass consciousness, has produced a great deal of detail and additional information which has, in order to preserve clarity, not been included in any of these books.

If any questions have come to mind in reading any, or all of these books, and they do not appear to be answered within the pages, then readers can write to the author at the address below. It will not be possible to answer all of your questions personally, but these questions and the answers will probably form the basis for a new book.

If you just feel like writing to me to agree, or better still to disagree, with what has been written, then please do so via the publishers.

I hope that these books have answered many of your questions and look forward to meeting you all after we have made our final transitions.

A selection of other Capall Bann titles. Free catalogue available.

The Healing Book   by Chris Thomas & Diane Baker

This book is for those who wish to heal, starting with simple exercises to unlock the healing potential which is inherent in all of us. Nobody needs to feel left out of these abilities. We are all healers, all that we need to do is to stop telling ourselves that we are not. Whatever level of experience you have of healing, this book explains in simple uncomplicated language how to understand the "Chakras" and the way in which our daily lives influence them, to relate medical conditions to the chakras and to learn methods which will bring the chakras back into balance, both for yourself and for others. These methods apply equally to humans and to animals. If you do not have any experience of giving healing, but would like to learn, this book can set you on that path. If you already work as a healer, in whatever capacity, and would like to explore your greater potential, this book is also for you. The authors have a combined experience of over twenty five years of providing healing and have taught very many people to unlock their own healing potential. This book is not only about learning to heal from the beginning, but also explores some of the energy manipulation techniques used by the authors in their daily practise as "Psychic Surgeons". ISBN 1 86163 053 0   £8.95

VORTEX - The End of History   by Mary Russell

This book is compiled of transmissions through the highly disciplined mediumship of Mary Russell. Some of the souls who have given of their knowledge and observations from the world unseen were household names in one or more of their past sojourns in human bodies. Others come from worlds different to ours. Their collective aim is to inform us as much as possible of what is real and what is not, distinguishing between intellectual fantasy and true eternal science, In doing this, they point out where we came from and where we are going. Much of their message is to do with the great changes now occurring as well as greater ones to come as this planet heads towards a vortex in time, centred around the year 1999. They are all designed to promote the progress of each human soul. The intelligence and the love in charge of it all, as glimpsed through these messages, is breathtaking and awesome in its grandeur. ISBN 1 86163 0832   £11.95

The Face of the Deep - Healing Body and Soul   by Penny Allen

We cannot truly heal our bodies or minds without recognising the needs of the soul. The healing process appears magical or miraculous only when we do not understand the inner workings behind life. Outer and inner are inseparable. Ancient gods share their names with the planets and their influences with colours, music, numbers and chakras, the energy wheels within our bodies. Penny Allen has a background as a journalist and a teacher of literature as well as twenty years of experience as a teacher of meditation and as a healer, counsellor and astrologer. Drawing on mythology, she leads us on a fascinating journey of discovery showing how the soul is linked to the body and mind and concluding that, if we are to heal ourselves and our environment, we must align ourselves once again to the universe of which we are part.
ISBN 1 86163 0409   £9.95

Medicine for the Coming Age   by Dr Lisa Sand

Dr Lisa Sand has long been aware of the presence of post-traumatic stress disorder in all souls incarnated on planet Earth. It is the major cause of physical, emotional, mental and spiritual disorders and symptoms. Their variations are myriad and distressing, but relief is great when the cause can be eliminated. Fear, anger and frustration give way to joyous life fulfilment. In the last 23 years, Dr Sand has devoted herself completely to this task, together with selected mediums who have been her earthly collaborators, and a number of wonderful, highly skilled souls who are not now incarnate, but who have been very active indeed in participating in the work from the point of their unlimited vision and vast experience with human souls. This book is a joint statement and description of the work by all concerned through the pen of Dr Sand. Its purpose is to help heal and enlighten all who read it. ISBN 1 86163 068 9   £9.95

FREE DETAILED CATALOGUE

A detailed illustrated catalogue is available on request, SAE c
International Postal Coupon appreciated. **Titles can be ordere**
direct from Capall Bann, post free in the UK (cheque or PO wit
order) or from good bookshops and specialist outlets. Titles current
available include:

Angels and Goddesses - Celtic Christianity & Paganism by Michael Howard
Arthur - The Legend Unveiled by C Johnson & E Lung
Auguries and Omens - The Magical Lore of Birds by Yvonne Aburrow
Book of the Veil The by Peter Paddon
Caer Sidhe - Celtic Astrology and Astronomy by Michael Bayley
Call of the Horned Piper by Nigel Jackson
Celtic Lore & Druidic Ritual by Rhiannon Ryall
Earth Dance - A Year of Pagan Rituals by Jan Brodie
Earth Magic by Margaret McArthur
Enchanted Forest - The Magical Lore of Trees by Yvonne Aburrow
Familiars - Animal Powers of Britain by Anna Franklin
Healing Homes by Jennifer Dent
Herbcraft - Shamanic & Ritual Use of Herbs by Susan Lavender & Anna Franklin
In Search of Herne the Hunter by Eric Fitch
Magical Guardians - Exploring the Spirit & Nature of Trees by Philip Heselton
Magical Lore of Cats by Marion Davies
Magical Lore of Herbs by Marion Davies
Masks of Misrule - The Horned God & His Cult in Europe by Nigel Jackson
Patchwork of Magic by Julia Day
Psychic Self Defence - Real Solutions by Jan Brodie
Sacred Animals by Gordon MacLellan
Sacred Grove - The Mysteries of the Forest by Yvonne Aburrow
Sacred Geometry by Nigel Pennick
Sacred Lore of Horses The by Marion Davies
Sacred Ring - Pagan Origins British Folk Festivals & Customs by Michael Howard
Seasonal Magic - Diary of a Village Witch by Paddy Slade
Secret Places of the Goddess by Philip Heselton
Talking to the Earth by Gordon Maclellan
Taming the Wolf - Full Moon Meditations by Steve Hounsome

Capall Bann is owned and run by people actively involved in many of the areas in which w
publish. Our list is expanding rapidly so do contact us for details on the latest releases.

Capall Bann Publishing, Auton Farm, Milverton, Somerset, TA4 1NE